Palmistry Hand in Hand

Palmistry Hand in Hand

A Guide to Western and Vedic Hand Reading

Beleta Greenaway

ZAMBEZI PUBLISHING LTD

Published in the UK in 2013
by Zambezi Publishing Ltd
P.O. Box 221 Plymouth,
Devon PL2 2YJ (UK)
Tel: +44 (0)1752 367 300
email: info@zampub.com
www.zampub.com

British Library Cataloguing in Publication Data:
A catalogue record for this book
is available from the British Library

ISBN: 978-1-903065-70-9

Illustrations © 2013 Malcolm Wright & Beleta Greenaway
Cover © 2013 Jan Budkowski

Printed & bound in the UK by Lightning Source (UK)

Disclaimer:- This book is intended to provide information regarding the subject matter, and to entertain.
The contents are not exhaustive and no warranty is given as to accuracy of content. The book is sold on the
understanding that neither the publisher not the author are thereby engaged in rendering professional
services, in respect of the subject matter or any other field. If expert guidance is required, the services of a
competent professional should be sought.

Readers are urged to access a range of other material on the book's subject matter, and to tailor the
information to their individual needs. Neither the author nor the publisher shall have any responsibility to
any person or entity regarding any loss or damage caused or alleged to be caused, directly or indirectly, by
the use or misuse of information contained in this book. If you do not wish to be bound by the above, you
may return this book in original condition to the publisher, with its receipt, for a refund of the purchase
price.

About the Author

Beleta Greenaway

Beleta grew up in a mystical family and learned both Western and Vedic palmistry when she was very young. She has worked as a consultant Hand Reader for over thirty years, and she teaches and runs workshops on the subject. Unusually, Beleta likes to use a combination of Eastern and Western methods in her palmistry, and she is an absolute master of both.

Besides being adept at various kinds of card reading, Beleta is also a clairvoyant with a deep knowledge of crystals, angels, spell-casting, spirituality, herbs and much more. She is also the author of Simply Angels. Notwithstanding her abilities, Beleta is the most down-to-earth person you could hope to meet.

Beleta is married to John and she has one daughter, Leanna.

Dedication

I dedicate this book to Catherine Coverdale. Thank you for your endless patience, help and support. You truly are a very special friend.

Many thanks to Sasha Fenton, my publisher, for her input and for making this book possible, but above all for having faith in my palmistry knowledge.

A special mention to Lynn Seal, a fabulous palmist whose ideas have been an inspiration to me.

A big thank you to my husband John Greenaway, for his love and support.

Contents

Introduction –
Palmistry Hand in Hand

Welcome to the magical world of palmistry. In a very short time, you will be able to amaze your friends and colleagues with your expertise and knowledge in the fascinating subject of hand analysis, but first let us look more closely at this ancient craft.

A Brief History

Chirology is another name for palmistry, or a study of the hands, and it probably originated in the Indian sub-continent; there are texts in Indian museums that go back over 5,000 years. However, written evidence doesn't always survive, so there may have been earlier texts than these, and an oral tradition that goes back even further.

Since the beginning of human history, the hand has enthralled and captivated all cultures and races. In addition to the Indians, the Chinese, Greeks and Persians were amongst the first civilizations openly to practice the art of Chirology, whilst the Egyptians were also known to have an avid interest in it, often combining palmistry with astrology. Judging by the number of painted hand pictures found in prehistoric caves, especially in France, Spain and Australia, it's apparent that some form of hand reading has been around since the beginning of time.

The chances are that palmistry, along with many other esoteric skills, moved westward as a result of the Crusades, which brought Westerners into close contact with Eastern countries and peoples. Later, palmistry became associated with gypsies and then fortunetellers.

Nomadic wanderers have brought their knowledge to many parts of Europe over the last three hundred years, and the old saying "cross my palm with silver" is quite probably the origin of paying for a reading.

As mentioned, there are references to palmistry in many ancient books ranging from the Bible to the Brahmanic Vedas and the Torah.

Sadly, palmistry was forced to go underground by the Catholic Church, which labelled the craft as the work of the devil. Those who were found to be practicing chiromancy were in danger of being murdered and disposed of secretly. Despite this, man's fascination with the hand flourished, and today, all over the world, there are people who still use this magical art, with many more eager to learn the skills.

The Journey of Life

Every time you look at the lines on someone's hand, you are looking at that person's journey of life and the map of their character and fate. Although palmistry is considered a science and each line on the palm represents a certain meaning, it is also known to be another channel for psychics to gain information, because touching or feeling the hand brings a vibration to the clairvoyant and thus becomes a form of psychometry. A true clairvoyant will be able to tune into the psychic vibration of their client (sometimes called the "Querent") when performing hand analysis, thus benefiting from both psychic and scientific aspects. Sometimes an initial letter will be clearly seen on the hand, and this can represent someone very important with that initial in their name, due to come into the life of the seeker. It could be a lover, a child, or a member of the seeker's family or friends. A house or an image might suddenly appear on the palm to give the palmist extra help in defining what is going on in that person's life. Another time, you might delve into the same hand and find that particular information has gone, which means the situation has passed.

Once, I was browsing the hand of a new client and saw the image of a tepee. I asked him if he had recently been to a North American Indian reservation. His head shot up in amazement as he had just returned from one the week before.

The Romany gypsies believe that the left hand is what God has given you and the right hand is what you do with the potential. In their readings, many modern chirologists will tell you that the left hand represents the past and that it can hold karmic knowledge of previous lives, while the right hand holds knowledge of the future. Of course, this assumes the person is right-handed, because, if the person is left-handed, the process is reversed.

Those who might want to become palmists will find the following lists helpful.

The Ten Do's and Don'ts of Palmistry

Do...
1. Find a calm and peaceful room for the consultation.
2. Set the mood by burning oil or incense of lavender or poppy "opium". These two fragrances can enhance psychic ability and create a peaceful ambiance.
3. Ensure that the readings are on a one-to-one basis.
4. Have a lamp or small spotlight on the table to illuminate gloomy days.
5. Purchase a good magnifying glass to see tiny lines. Some have a light included.
6. You might wish to have your favourite crystal nearby on the table.
7. Remember your client is the most important person during their reading.
8. Practise on friends and family, taking their handprints to study. A good photocopy of their hand can be helpful if you want to avoid the mess of the ink.
9. Wash your hands before and after every consultation. You may prefer a medical hand gel. You might find that each person will have his or her own special vibration or energy, and with practice, you could link into this.
10. Turn off all telephones and try not to interrupt the reading, as that stems the flow.

Don't...
1. Have radios or TVs playing in the room that you work in while you're giving a consultation.
2. Don't have children or pets running around when working.
3. Make any hair-raising predictions. If in doubt, say nowt!
4. Become a "party piece". People will love to ask you to dinner and bombard you with questions. I once arrived to have dinner with a new "friend" and found she had invited four of her friends as well, and I was the unwitting entertainment for the evening!
5. Be put off making a recording of your reading for a client. Many get comfort from them, and some people have bad memories.
6. EVER read for a strange man if you are a female and if you are alone in the house. You might be asking for trouble. A few years ago, I did a full hour reading for a young man who sat in captivated

silence. After the reading, he pounced on me! Luckily, I manage to throw him out on the street. It is best to ask a friend or a family member to be around if needed.

7. Discuss your private life with your client. This is extremely unprofessional and could add weight to their burdens, as well as making you vulnerable to con artists.

8. Ever divulge information from other people's readings. Every reading must be in complete and utter confidence. Remember, you will hold many secrets and often will read for large families, celebrities and folk in all professional walks of life.

9. Be fazed by the variety of clientele you may meet, and be prepared to be flexible in your outlook. Treat everyone equally.

10. Ever discuss or criticise other well-known clairvoyants to your clients. This is extremely unprofessional. Many people visit many different psychics for fun and entertainment, and you can bet your life that anything you say will be repeated.

However, after all of the do's and don'ts, do remember to enjoy your newfound hobby or career.

Quick Reminders

Chirology	Palmistry
Palmistry	The interpretation of the hand or the technique of reading hands
Chirognomy	The study of hand shapes, finger formations and the textures of the skin
Chiromancy	Reading the lines on the palms

1: Tools of the Trade

Large Magnifying Glass
Buy the largest one you can find and ensure that it is good quality. There are some nice ones with battery lighting attached that will help to make the lines even more visible, especially on dimly lit days or dark evenings. If possible, keep it stored in a velvet pouch or bag when not in use, because the glass can easily become scratched. Keep a soft cloth in the bag to polish the glass every now and again.

Small Halogen Lamp
I find this useful when doing evening party readings, or you might prefer a small torch.

Fine Pens
There are times when you will want to point out clearly a line or mark on your client's hand, so a fine pointed, felt tipped pen can be used to trace the lines.

Taking Prints
You will need the following items:
» A tube of water-based printing ink. The most suitable is Dahler-Rowney ink. It is quite hard to locate in shops, but the Internet is a good place to find it. I usually order the larger tubs, which last longer. The usual colour to use is black, but you may prefer another dark colour. As a last resort, you can use a dark lipstick to cover the hands. It is messy, but can have excellent results if you're careful not to smudge the print. I have seen other palmists use acrylic paint quite successfully, too.
» An old plate, tray or tile for spreading the ink into an even substance.
» A paste up roller or a small sponge paint roller from a DIY shop, an art shop or online.

» A cosmetic sponge.

» A4 white paper or thin card.

» A4 thin sponge pad or a thin pile of sheets of kitchen roll.

The Method

Place the A4 paper onto the sponge pad or kitchen paper and secure with a few pins on each corner. Squeeze a small amount of ink onto the plate and roll it until you get a good flat consistency on the roller. Roll the ink onto the palm, fingers and thumb, making sure the wrist area (rascettes) are also inked, because they hold vital information. Use the cosmetic sponge to dab the hand all over to make the ink even. You may wish to take several prints for each client, with some showing one area of the hand and others showing different areas.

Place the client's hand centrally on the paper and gently press down on each finger, putting light pressure on the phalanges. Try not to smudge or smear the print, as you will need it as clean as possible. Next press the inner palm down firmly, and also use the same procedure for the rascettes. If the palm is very hollow, take a small pad of kitchen paper and place it under the portion of paper covering the hollow part of the palm.

To get a good print of the rascettes, gently lift the fingers and palm up, ask your client slowly to roll the wrist from side to side to cover all of the lines. You might decide to do the rascettes independently on a separate piece of paper. Ink the percussion (the side of the hand opposite the thumb) up to the top edge of the Mercury finger and gently roll this area from side to side on the paper to get full coverage. It is a good idea to do the fingerprints separately as well as the full print.

When you have a full set of hand prints completed, draw carefully around the fingers and hand shape with a medium felt-tipped pen, name and date it and leave it to dry for about an hour. It is a good idea to photocopy the print as a back up. Placing it in a plastic folder will protect it from any harm.

If you decide not to have an ink print and prefer a photocopy print, make sure you don't press the hand down too hard in the photocopier, as you will get white, featureless marks. You might find you need help to get your own print done and make sure you also copy the back of the hand to see the nails as they offer a great deal of information on health issues. Many palmists will use colour photocopying as well as the traditional black and white.

2: The Basics

There are four major hand shapes:
- » Air
- » Earth
- » Fire
- » Water

Novice palmists often become mystified when they try to match the hand shape with the birth sign of the individual, because it doesn't always follow. For instance, I was born under the sign of Aquarius, which is an air sign, but I have a fire hand. My advice when judging personalities from palm readings is to concentrate solely on the hand shape, as this seems to be the most accurate.

The Air Hand
Also known as the philosophical hand
The palm is square and a little shorter than the fingers. There will be plenty of lines present in the palm. The skin texture is usually smooth and firm.

Air hand

Meaning
Air palm people love company, so socialising will be at the top of their agenda. They have many different types of friends and they can change like a chameleon to accommodate them all. They are deep thinking intellectuals who love animals and who want to put right the injustices of the world. You might find them working for good causes that will help mankind. These individuals have methodical and tidy minds, but this isn't always reflected in the way they keep their home or offices. They love detail, delight in research and history, and their intellect is usually superior to others. As their nature is all about reflection and deliberation, they won't be rushed into anything.

In love
The air hand person will want lots of communication from their partner as well as sex. Although their libido is quite high, friendship will be more important in the long run.

Negative traits
At times these types will be opinionated and nitpick about everything. Because they are so critical and can be scathing, they are hard to live with. They often have a chip on their shoulders. Sometimes they can be cold and calculating and will often play mind games.

The Earth Hand
Practical hand
The palm is square, with stocky fingers and a firm skin texture. The palm and fingers are both short. As a rule there will be fewer lines on this type of hand than the other types.

Meaning
Earth hand people are dependable, stoic and hard working, and their feet are planted firmly on the ground. If they are in repetitive work, they won't mind too much and they will put in lots of effort. They have a truly honest personality and believe in fair play. If I were to employ someone, then this type of hand would be the one I would choose, because its owner will be very conscientious in all they do. The earth hand person will love to be out of doors; they often grow their own vegetables and have a sense of pride in providing for the family. When they retire, many seek solitude in the country and perhaps will own a

Earth hand

smallholding with chickens, ducks and geese. They also love cats and dogs, so they could end up with a bit of a menagerie.

In love
Earth hand owners are romantic. They love sex and won't have many inhibitions. They adore food, soft lights and drawn curtains, a fine bottle of wine and a good film on the television. If they can cuddle up with their chosen companion for the evening, they will be perfectly happy and content.

Negative traits
These people are stubborn and can be ill at ease or gauche in company. Some are often tongued tied and shy. If their mind is fixed on something, then they will be blinkered to all persuasion, especially if the thumb is broad and stout.

The Fire Hand
Artistic
The palm should be considerably longer than the fingers and there will be plenty of lines on the palm. Often the colour will be slightly rosier than other hand types and the hand will be warm to the touch. A good fire hand will have a bold Mount of Venus and a strong Mars Mount.

Fire hand

Meaning

These people are on the ball and are good judges of character. They live for the moment and gain what they can as it comes along. Fire hands are psychic and can read minds, so you need to guard your thoughts from them. Their motto is Carpe Diem... seize the day.

Owners of this hand are usually very active types who love excitement and action. Fun loving and enthusiastic, they enjoy exploring. They will prefer to be the boss and will frequently run their own businesses. The fire hand types will be artistic and warm hearted, and will rely on their intuition.

In love

When in love, fire hand people can be ardent and have a high libido. In the bedroom, they can be inventive and will find sex toys and saucy videos a hoot. The male owner of a fire hand will often laugh his lady into bed. Before getting married, they will have quite a few partners, but when they settle down they will be very loyal.

Negative traits

Fire hands can be noisy and rush from one thing to another, expending their energies on trivia. As they can sometimes be overbearing and attention-seeking, they lack real friendships and often end up lonely.

Water hand

The Water Hand

Psychic

The palm is long, as are the fingers. Some say this is the most psychic of all hands. There will be a myriad of lines in the palm, which can be a nightmare for the palmist when trying to analyse it.

Meaning

Water hand owners are dreamy, mysterious and psychic. The phases of the Moon can affect them and the moon mount will be well developed on these types of hands. The Neptune mount should be rounded, too. Water hands show good creative abilities and these people make wonderful friends and great parents.

In love

As they are dreamy, they will love the formality of courtship, poetry and long romantic walks in the countryside. Secret trysts and romantic letters appeal to them. Often they are too romantic and vulnerable. Their high ideals will often come crashing around them, ultimately causing heartbreak.

Negative traits

Water hands can be possessive, manipulative and revengeful. They never forget past hurts. Indeed they NEVER forget anything!

Mixed Hands

Often one will come across a hand that does not fit into the four categories. The left hand might be fire and the right hand might be earth. If the person is right-handed, then you should use the character in the left hand for the past personality and the right hand for the future development. Sometimes the hand shapes vary so much that no decision can be made, and you will have to look at other factors on the palm to help you. In time, experience will give you a feel for what is right.

Meaning

This character will be multi-talented, a jack-of-all-trades and they will most likely have several careers. They can be witty, quick thinking and very astute.

In love

I have found mixed hand types can be quite promiscuous. They like variation and can be in love with two or three people at the same time. Their restless nature can prevent long and lasting relationships. On the plus side, because of their sexual experiences, they make very good lovers.

Negative traits

They can be like will-of the-wisps, unable to settle down and end up drifting from one place to another. They rarely finish a project and can be a nightmare for partners, as they will constantly want to move homes and jobs.

Fingers and Palms the Same Length

When this formation is present the person will be well balanced, reliable and level headed. They enjoy studying and work, but will also like time away from employment. Being adaptable, they often have a variety of careers during their lifetime and are usually successful in all of them. They have a brilliant sense of humour and because of that, they are popular.

Broad Palms

These types are very loving and steady, especially in marriage. They are "older souls" and so have great wisdom, sympathy and depth. Broad palm people are popular and others seek their advice. They choose roles to help society, and if they have the Medical Striata on their hands (see the chapter on minor lines), could become doctors, nurses or some kind of health practitioners.

They have energy, drive and ambition, but also like to please others. If children have broad palms, they are rarely naughty and will sometimes seem older than their years.

Narrow Palms

This type of palm can sometimes belong to narrow-minded people. The owner will find it hard to be generous. If they are to purchase a gift for someone, they will look for a bargain, while at the same time treating themselves to something expensive. Some narrow-palmed folk can have a cruel streak and find it hard to socialise, especially in groups.

However, you must take account of the fact that if you are studying the hand of a slim, short person, this type of palm will be completely normal for them in a positive way.

FLEXIBILITY OF THE HAND

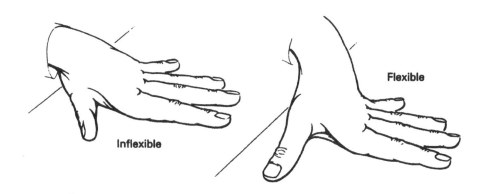

Inflexible

Flexible

Flexible Hands

This person is restless and can soon lose interest in a project, sometimes not completing what they have started. They will need lots of stimulation, and when younger, can be a handful for their parents.

Inflexible Hands

These are sedentary types who love routine and prefer to stay at home in front of the television. Often they are unfeeling and cold with a rigid outlook to life. They will isolate themselves and do anything for a quiet life.

Claw Shaped Hands

Claw shaped hands look like talons, and their owners tend to be greedy, with critical natures and sharp tongues. Often they are difficult to please; no matter how hard you try, they will never be satisfied and will make those close to them feel inadequate.

3: The Sections of the Hand

A useful tip in palmistry is to look at the hand in three parts. It makes the synopsis easier and more accurate to predict. Palmists will take a print of the hand and then divide it into three sections to get a broader picture of their client.

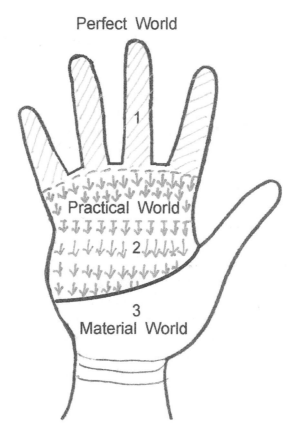

The Three Sections of the Hand

The Perfect World
Section one shows the top of the fingers tapering down to the base of the fingers. This helps us to understand the person's hopes, dreams and ambitions and how they view the world and their spiritual life.

Well Formed Fingers
If the fingers (especially the Saturn finger) are well formed, it shows the person is well balanced. Taking a tape measure, find out if this is the longest section of the hand; if it is, your subject will enjoy academic study and will have a thirst for learning. He will literally be a walking encyclopaedia and a wonderful teacher. If this part of the hand is shorter, then the opposite applies.

The Practical World
This is the middle section of the hand and reveals a wealth of knowledge. It runs from the base of the fingers and encompasses both lower and higher Mars Mounts and the Quadrangle.

Wide Space
When this is the deepest and widest part of the palm, we have an owner who will be very practical and able to put his hand to most things. These people will usually have their own business, which will run like clockwork. They can be quite inventive, especially if they are in the building trade, and they can be a Jack-of-all-trades. These folk are the salt of the earth. They are efficient and good timekeepers.

The Material World
This formation runs from the bottom of the Mars mounts and encompasses the mount of Venus, the Neptune mount and the rascettes.

If this is the more pronounced area of the hand, these people will want financial security above everything else. They consider their own desires and needs and while they can talk the talk and walk the walk, when it boils down to it, they put themselves first every time. If the space is balanced and not too heavy, the individual will enjoy cash but not allow it to rule them, and they will be hard working, tenacious and kind.

THE RADIAL AND ULNA SIDES OF THE PALM

The radial side is located on the thumb side and the ulna is on the opposite, percussion side. When studying the palm, we look for balance and harmony, and by splitting the hand in half we can see more clearly if there are any flaws or outstanding attributes. Sometimes it is better to work systematically on one portion of the palm rather than drifting the eyes over the whole picture.

Sasha Fenton, who is also a palmist, suggests it is a good idea to take a piece of paper and lay it onto the hand so that it covers the ulna side and just look at the radial side. Then do the same with the ulna side. This shows that there is a distinct difference in the size of a hand from one side to the other. Note the two different ways in which you can divide the hand.

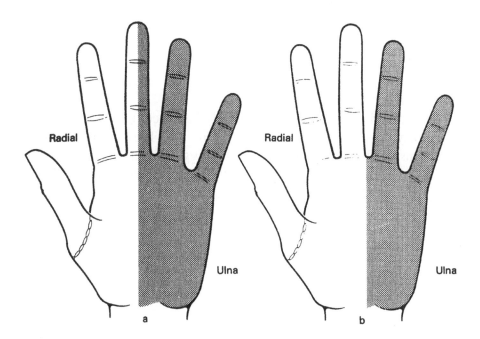

The Radial Side of the Palm

This represents the face the person presents to the world, and a good radial shows the individual will be confident, materialistic and outgoing. They will enjoy the cut and thrust of the business world, and money will be important to them.

A Pronounced Radial

Those who have pronounced radials are ambitious and energetic; the world is their oyster and they strive to do well at everything. These people are competitive and materialistic. Their lack of spiritual belief can make them seem rather shallow. Their sex drive will be high, but they will lack the tenderness of a true lover and will soon move on to the next challenge, as they love variety. These people are assertive in business and although ruthless, can be fair and generous bosses.

Pronounced Ulna

People with this formation are vulnerable and emotional. They yearn to paint, draw and write, but their lack of confidence will hold them back, so their efforts usually result in failure. They are indecisive and will often let others make decisions for them, becoming resentful and dissatisfied with their lives when it doesn't work out. It is quite rare to see a pronounced ulna however, because the majority of people have a more balanced hand.

Equal Balance

When both sides of the palm are equally balanced, the owners will be fairly easy going and will enjoy life to the full. They are kind, have a good sense of humour, and can see the bigger picture in life. Because they have many talents, from the scientific to the creative, and lead a happy family life, they enjoy their lives to the full.

4: The Percussion or Ulna Edge of the Hand

The percussion section of the hand tells us a lot about the nature and character of the person and also the places they might visit in the world. Health issues can sometime show up here, too. The following diagrams will help you to ascertain the different types you might encounter.

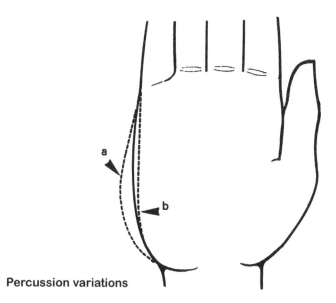

Percussion variations

Flat Percussion (b)

If the side of the percussion appears flat and thin on its outline, the owner of this hand will often have no stamina or staying power. Perhaps their energy levels will come in fits and starts, and they need to have plenty of rest and pauses to recharge their batteries. Sometimes their libido is quite low.

Low Bulbous Percussion

The lower percussion will be quite dominant in sporty types. The owners of this type of hand will be out-going, living on their adrenalin, enjoying sports and outdoor pursuits. Their libido will be high and they can be quite promiscuous until they find their true love. As they are restless, they must have plenty of variety in their lives. Often they will take jobs that involve travel or exploration, and they like to get off the beaten track. Others could successfully choose acting or dancing as a career.

The Middle Bulbous Percussion (a)

These subjects are attractive, amusing, intuitive and highly creative, and they can captivate an audience with their fascinating personality. This is a psychic hand, and those who are not sure of their gift or who are in denial of this gift, might have to be encouraged to pay attention to their dream sleep and to record their dreams. It would also be a good idea for them to attend meditation and self-awareness groups. On the whole, they should already be on their path and will often be clairvoyant and into esoteric and holistic pursuits.

Rounded Percussion

These folk live on their nerves and are very highly-strung, fidgety, and restless. They can lack concentration. Often they will miss out on today, because they will be worrying about tomorrow. As a whole, they will benefit from such things as meditation, yoga or an aromatherapy session.

Full Percussion

Whenever you see a full percussion, the owners of this hand will be highly imaginative and sensitive, with scant regard for material possessions. They make good writers, especially if there is a trident on the end of the headline.

Boxed Percussion

This is similar to the square shaped hand, so these folks thrive on hard work and outdoor activities. They will sometimes neglect relationships, because they will often be workaholics. On the plus side, they are great fun to be with, but can be a little staid in the bedroom.

Thick and Thin Percussions

Those with thick percussions can cope with a lot of stress, as nothing seems to faze them. If the edge is thin, then the opposite applies. The owners can be sensitive, easily hurt, and upset.

5: The Knuckles

Ask your client to make a fist without gripping too hard, and then ask them to hold their arms down so that you can see the knuckles clearly. Look at the back of the hand to see if one knuckle stands out as being larger than the rest. When a person gets older, the knuckles can sometimes swell with arthritis or rheumatism, so that must be taken into consideration when reading the hand.

Larger Jupiter Knuckle

As this finger represents a subject's image, self-confidence and ego, large Jupiter knuckles show good self-esteem, and individuals would do well if self-employed. When over-large, these types can be prone to arrogance.

Small Jupiter Knuckle

These owners will lack confidence and be easily led. They dislike having to think for themselves and hang back in the workplace, refusing to take responsibility.

Large Saturn Knuckle

The Saturn finger represents everyday life, our responsibilities and also our consciousness. Those who have large Saturn knuckles are responsible types and think hard about their day- to-day activities. If they say they will do something, they do it rather than let others down. These individuals are good leaders and fair bosses, which makes them popular. Over-large knuckles belong to folk who are inclined to restrict themselves by conforming to rigid rules.

Small Saturn Knuckle
These types care little for others and will always look for the easy way out. They hate responsibility and will take a long time to grow up. Because of their immaturity, their relationships can be a nightmare.

Large Apollo Knuckle
This is the finger of optimism and creativity. When the Apollo knuckles are the largest on the hand, it signifies those who are captivated by art of any sort. They love to work in areas of creativity, they will have a good eye for fashion and interior design, and they may sit for hours using their skills with cake crafting, card making and sewing. If the knuckle is very dominant, there will be a wonderful flair present and the owner might find media fame.

Small Apollo Knuckle
There will be little interest in art or craft, although they will love to visit galleries and might well have an interest in fashion. They will, however, lack the creative skills to develop their own style.

Large Mercury Knuckle
Mercury represents oration, communication and truth. A large Mercury knuckle is indicative of the gift for speech or perhaps a lovely singing voice, which can captivate others. Its owner hates to tell lies and will be a seeker of truth. As they enjoy company they will feel at home in a group or large family setting. If the knuckle is over-large, the person will star in some sort of television or media work.

Small Mercury Knuckle
This person could be shy and a little tongue-tied. They love to mix with others, but stay in the background rather than get too involved. Sometimes they will have trouble expressing themselves artistically and they constantly put themselves down.

Smooth Knuckles
When all of the knuckles are smooth and of the same proportions, the owner will be psychic, impulsive and day-dreamy.

Knotted Knuckles

Those who have knuckles that are knotted and deeply grooved are inclined to have tunnel vision and don't like to be told anything. They tend to be know-alls who may enjoy forcing their opinions on others.

Under Developed Knuckles

Low self-esteem comes with this formation, and the owner will have a painfully shy nature. They will be kind and generous, and, as my grandmother would say, "the better for knowing". Sometimes they suffer a little with their health as they have a delicate constitution.

Full Range

When the knuckles are a full range with plenty of peaks and valleys, the person will enjoy good health and stamina.

6: The Topography of the Hand – The Mounts

Holding your hand in front of you, look down across the palm to see the mounts. Larger mounts signify more vitality, caused by brain energy flowing into them. Consider the mounts as hills, the Plain of Mars the valley and the lines as rivers and inlets.

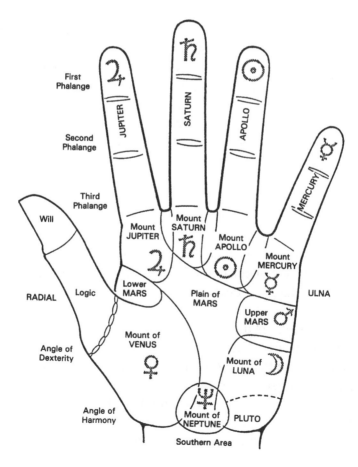

The Venus Mount

This mount is set on the fleshy part of the thumb and it is the largest mount on the hand. It represents love, passion, libido and emotion. The family and friendship areas are to be found here too, as are gifts in the social arts.

Large, red Venus mounts belong to those who are over-fond of food and alcohol, and who like their creature comforts. They can be obsessive about sex and will seek new ways to keep their libido energised. These types are sometimes referred to as "body people".

Medium Venus mounts represent a good balance. These types enjoy the finer aspects of life, as well as enjoying a happy and contented home life where they will make steady and caring parents.

Those with a flat or hard Venus mount have quite cold natures and can be difficult to get to know, as their characters are rather shallow. They don't always enjoy good health, have a lack of resistance to germs and sometimes a poor appetite. My grandmother, who taught me old-fashioned palmistry, used to say these individuals are prone to being frigid. Narrow and flat mount types are sometimes called "mind people". A narrow Mount of Venus doesn't denote a lack of interest in sex, although it does indicate an inability to give and receive love easily. A cramped and flat Venus shows an active mind and a person who will fantasise about sex rather than enact it.

In short, the bon-viveur has the large Venus mount while the aesthete has the smaller one.

The Jupiter Mount

The Jupiter mount sits at the base of the index or Jupiter finger and when over-large, these folk are inclined to expend too much energy on projects that won't get finished. Gambling might be an interest and they take chances for the sheer hell of it. As they have a taste for the good things in life and a great deal of vanity, their lives can be like a tangled ball of string.

Those who have medium-sized Jupiter mounts are enterprising and become good leaders. They have an ambitious streak. As bosses, they will be fair and like to bring out the best in their staff. They hate bullies. As they have a thirst for knowledge and an interest in languages, they will often study and take exams, even into old age.

When the Jupiter mount is flat, the owner can have low self-esteem and seek out friends who are happy to tell them what to do. They will cling to the family unit and will need others to make decisions for them. Because they take a long time to grow up, they will often lack skills in practical things and have low standards. Many are clumsy, untidy and forgetful.

The Saturn Mount

The Saturn mount sits at the base of the middle finger, and it is often a flat area or even a valley rather than an actual mount. However, hands vary tremendously, so actual mounts do appear here on occasion. In old-fashioned palmistry, this was classed as the health mount, which is associated with the bones, teeth, spleen and gall bladder. In some ways, I feel it is better not to have too strong a Saturn mount.

Over-large Saturn mounts suggest pessimism and sombre, doom-and-gloom types. When in the company of these people, others feel they have to cheer them up, as they tend to be such wet blankets. These people can sometimes have an interest in the black arts.

Medium-sized Saturn mounts denote those who are constructive. These subjects enjoy meditation, getting messages during dream-sleep and receiving prophesies. They may believe in UFOs, angels, the spirit world and anything that is New Age rather than religious. Often they will work as healers, aromatherapists and spiritual coaches.

Flat Saturn mounts are better than raised ones as they indicate well-balanced individuals with a wide outlook on life. Their motto will be *Carpe Diem* ... seize the day! An optimistic nature will usually bring benefits to this sort, because what they send out, they get back thrice fold.

The Apollo Mount

Some palmists call this the Mount of the Sun. Either way, it's the mount under the ring or Apollo finger. I class it as a happy mount, as there are so many good things that surround it.

Large Apollo mounts represent people who are talented, inspired and probably connected with the media or fame. They will shine in anything they pursue which might be dance, art, music and writing, while fate will give them lashings of help along the way. Also, with this formation the owner will love children and parenting.

Medium Apollo mount owners have magnetism, flair and a sense of fun. They will lighten a party, bring laughter and will have original ideas.

When the Apollo mount is flat, the owner will lack social graces and can be somewhat gauche. As if to compensate for their lack of talent, they will have a misguided sense of their own importance. These are the kinds of people we see on talent shows who are puffed up and full of self-esteem, only to be knocked down and brought into the real world. Their worst faults are being pompous and attention seeking.

The Mercury Mount

The Mercury mount is found at the base of the little finger and it leans toward the percussion side of the hand. The Mercury mount represents intellect, brainpower and a thirst for knowledge.

People who have large Mercury mounts have, so to speak, large brain-boxes. Ask them a question and you have your own personal encyclopaedia. They will know exactly where Macchu Picchu is on the map and they may even have been there, because they love to travel. They have an appetite for science and will often make wonderful teachers. They are quick witted, funny and good communicators.

When the Mercury mount is medium in size the owners will take an interest in their health and make sure they get plenty of fresh air and vitamins. You can't fool them, because they are very shrewd and can see through you, and spot your problems and faults in an instant. If the Mercury finger is pointed with a medium mount, we have psychic powers present in the owner.

A low Mercury mount is often found on the hands of those who, as children, had difficulties when learning to read or write and were slower at school than their peer group. They will be a little clumsy and prone to silly accidents and forgetfulness. Their nature will still be positive, but the nervous system will often let them down.

The Luna Mount

This is also known as the Moon Mount and it is located on the lower percussion, just above the wrist. As the moon is very mysterious, so is this mount. The old-fashioned palmists, like gypsies, would study this in great detail.

A large Luna mount represents an interest in all things mystic and psychic, such as tarot cards, runes and divination, while trance work connected to mediumship will fascinate them. Many clairvoyants have a raised Luna mount that can often be quite a deep pink colour.

A medium Luna mount owner will love water and especially the sea. Often these types will be affected by the moon cycles and will not be able to sleep if the moon is new or full. They tend to seek jobs connected to the sea, such as the navy, the merchant navy and working on cruise ships. Some will take work as fisherman, divers and oilrig workers. At the very least, they will love to travel.

When the Luna mount is flat, the person will have little intuition and a more practical nature, preferring to stick to well-known methods. If at all religious, they will keep to the strict teachings of the church. They will, however, have a protective instinct for their loved ones and will love animals.

The Neptune Mount
A large Neptune mount is quite rare. It is placed just above the wrist and is small and round, like a button.

A large Neptune mount will give protection on the water, so palmists like to see this with fishermen and navy personnel. Owners of a large mount will seek holistic and esoteric knowledge, and could have jobs in homeopathic practices, reflexology, shiatsu, aromatherapy and hypnosis.

A medium Neptune mount belongs on the hands of those who come into such things later on in their lives, perhaps after having a more conventional job. They will soon catch up and might practice the healing arts right up until old age.

When the Neptune Mount is flat, this would be classed as quite normal. It does not portray anything bad, just a normal attitude to mainstream life.

The Lower Mount of Mars
This mount sits in towards the percussion side of the hand, below the head line and in the Quadrangle. It is associated with resistance.

Large Lower Mount of Mars
Those who have a large lower Mars mount are courageous and may choose to work in the police force, the fire service, as paramedics or in the armed services. Females have tenacity and strength, sometimes out-performing a man.

Medium Lower Mount of Mars

Medium lower Mars mounts predict a rational view of life, someone who can do things on the spur of the moment and whose ideas often turn out well. They have lively personalities and will always stay motivated. We often find this type of person will gravitate towards self-employment.

Flat Lower Mount of Mars

Flat lower Mars mounts people show a lack of energy, are not aggressive and can often end up being bullied or put upon. Health-wise, there might be conditions with the blood, adrenal glands and kidneys.

Upper Mount of Mars

This mount sits in between the forefinger and the thumb.

Large Upper Mount of Mars

A large upper Mars mount shows good recovery from illness and great stamina. These individuals don't like being inactive; they enjoy getting on with life. They don't sit still for more than five minutes, so they can be restless and bad tempered if illness keeps them tethered.

According to the well-known palmist, Malcolm Wright, a large upper Mars mount belongs on the hands of those who like being in the armed forces and other organisations such as the scouts, guides and sea cadets. Both my own and Sasha's experience as palmists has born this out.

Medium Upper Mount of Mars

Medium upper Mars mounts show up on those who have stamina and will power and they will not often stray off the beaten path. They are somewhat righteous and single-minded, but will have good hearts. Over the three decades I have been a palmist, I have often noticed this formation on the palms of lawyers, magistrates and prison officers.

Flat Upper Mount of Mars

Flat upper Mars mounts denote low stamina and little resistance to any bugs going about. These people will take time to heal and need plenty of sleep.

THE PLAIN OF MARS

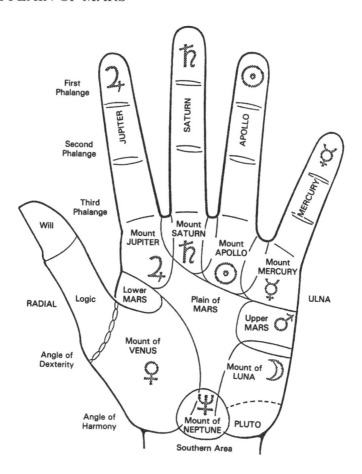

The Plain of Mars sits in the central part of the palm and tells us a lot about the personality of the seekers, also about their trials and tribulations. Most of the major lines of the hand pass through this triangular space, so ancient Vedic palmists would spend hours studying this area to gain maximum information.

When this area is crossed with fragmented lines, crosses, grilles and squares, the owners will face huge obstacles in their lives. Many of these problems will be caused by their own lack of judgement and immaturity, which in turn will make life difficult for their families and partners. I have found in my experience as a palmist that these types are not good at managing money and seldom hold down a job for long. They may rely on others to get them out of trouble and will often sponge off friends and family. If the Plain of Mars is blemish-free, then the subjects will be level headed, healthy and will put their backs into life.

The Pond
If the central palm is hollow, this is referred to as "the pond". Often when this formation is present, the owners will be low on energy, not sleeping well or recovering from an illness. When health is restored, the pond will often plump up to show that their vitality has returned.

Triangular Plain of Mars
When there is an obvious triangular shape in the Plain of Mars, these individuals are suffering from suppressed anger and resentment. Their moods will be unpredictable and they can suddenly lash out. This area will be red, blotchy and slightly damp. These types have many hang-ups and insecurities and some may have a slightly perverted nature.

A Bony Plain of Mars
When the Plain of Mars is wafer thin and under-developed, these people will lack confidence in their outward appearance and their inner talents and abilities. Sometimes these characters can be very good actors, hiding an inner shyness whilst presenting a brave face to the world.

Over-Developed Plain of Mars
This will sit quite high up in the palm, and its texture can be hard and fleshy. The owners will be thick skinned and lacking in manners. They don't listen to good advice and will have to learn by their mistakes. In Vedic palmistry, this character would be classed as "a young soul" who has much to learn.

7: Major Lines

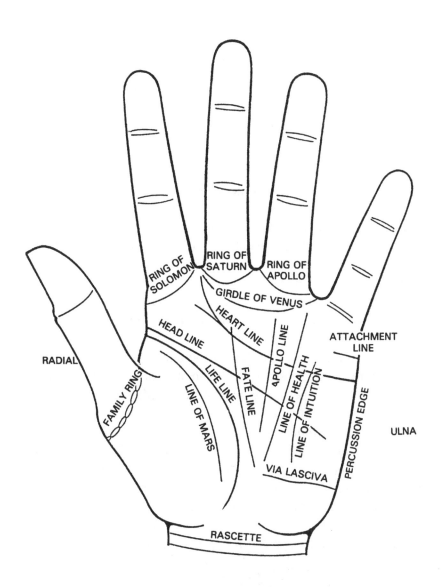

RING OF SOLOMON

RING OF SATURN

RING OF APOLLO

GIRDLE OF VENUS

HEART LINE

HEAD LINE

APOLLO LINE

ATTACHMENT LINE

RADIAL

FAMILY RING

LIFE LINE

FATE LINE

LINE OF HEALTH

LINE OF INTUITION

PERCUSSION EDGE

ULNA

LINE OF MARS

VIA LASCIVA

RASCETTE

The Life Line

The life line is the most vital line on the hand and holds huge importance to palmists. It starts between the Jupiter finger and thumb, and circles around the fleshy part of the Mount of Venus, often heading down towards the Rascettes of Venus for its termination point. Older palmistry traditions tell us that the life line can reveal the length of life. It certainly reveals the condition of our health, including such things as accidents and our management of health problems. Travel can also be seen on this line.

A Short Or Broken Life line

A short life line often depicts a major change of life at some point, after which the individual's life will be very different. Frequently, after the line stops, its energies are transferred to an extra line, which may be a recycled and reversed part of the fate line. I say recycled and reversed, because the fate line normally rises up the hand towards the fingers, but when the lower part takes over the job of the life line, you have to read that section of it downwards.

Sometimes the life line is weak, broken or even missing in parts, but the head line strengthens by way of compensation, and takes over some of the work of the life line.

While on the subject of strange life lines, Sasha remembers one lady who had no life line at all on her non-dominant hand, and asked her if anything life-threatening had happened to her. This lady told her that she had been in a terrible accident at the age of four and had not been expected to live, but modern medicine had done its magic and she recovered and lived a perfectly normal life thereafter.

Sasha also tells the following story:

"I once read the hands of a married couple whose life lines finished in the same place, with the classical 'move to the fate line' image stamped upon them. I told them they could both expect some major changes that would be sudden and dramatic, and it would happen to both of them at about the same time. This is what occurred. Some time after the reading, the chap was at work one day and came down with a migraine headache, so he decided to finish early and go home. When he

arrived home, his headache must have got much worse, because he discovered his wife in bed with someone else! Needless to say, life changed in that instant for both of them!"

Key Points

Try not to predict the exact length of someone's life, even if all the indications on the hand suggest a short life span. Also take into consideration that the left hand is what is given and the right hand is what you do with it. If a person is left handed, then this process is reversed.

My mother, Betty, had quite a long life line on her left hand, going somewhere towards the mid-eighties, but her right hand told a very different story, as it predicted that she would not live to see old age. She had been a heavy smoker since being a teenager and this caught up with her, so that she died at the age of fifty-nine from lung cancer. I have often given stern warnings when reading for smokers and I'm inclined not to hold back, especially if there is a narrowing in the central quadrangle, which can predict emphysema or asthmatic problems. On the brighter side, I have also saved lives with these warnings.

Can A Short Life Line Grow As We Get Older?

Yes it can. My husband John had a very short but vital life line and judging by the time scale on his hand, according to old palmistry traditions, he should have gone to meet his maker at about thirty-five years of age. Over the years, his life line has steadily grown and become quite strong. Vedic palmists believe if you are sad or unsettled, the life line can be short and thin, but when there is a purpose and thirst for life, the life line becomes stronger and longer.

Does A Break In The Life Line Mean The End?

No it doesn't. A break in a life line can mean, "off with the old and on with the new". If there is no cross on either broken line, then it bodes well. If a cross is present, then there might be an accident or sudden setback for the individual. If a square sits around the cross, then protection will be given.

Long Clear Life Lines

This can mean good health and sturdy vitality and such people bounce back from illness quickly. They will happily meet the challenges that come their way and will have lots of energy, even when they go into old age.

Sexy Life Lines

If the life line is especially red, then a passionate nature will be present and the individual will have a healthy libido.

Sick Life Lines

Sometimes you can see the life line is lack-lustre and very thin and fragmented, especially if the hand has a satiny shine to it; this means fatigue and sickness. Tassels will be present, or chains and grilles cutting across the life line, giving it an untidy appearance and a lack of conformity.

High Life Lines

These start quite high on the mount of Jupiter and show a driven nature that will do anything to succeed. These types will be highly ambitious and enjoy the cut and thrust of competition and business. They will have many irons in the fire and will have a thirst for intellectual interests. They will often further their education when older, going on to get a degree later in life.

Low Life Lines

A life line that starts just above the thumb suggests a personality that is uncomplicated and without ambition. The owners will prefer to live a simple life with their creature comforts and small circle of friends and family around them. They will have plenty of energy though, and will be on the go most of the time, but won't like to dwell too much on intellectual pursuits.

Common Life Lines

When the line starts between the Jupiter finger and the thumb there is a well-balanced aspect. These people will be eager to pursue life with a good degree of common sense and optimism. They will not want to be the best or the worst at anything, and such subjects will be ready for what fate offers. These people make laid-back parents who encourage their offspring in all things pertaining to education and hobbies.

8: The Head Line

The head line tells us how an individual thinks, and it shows their mental ability. It also tells a great deal about the path of their career, finances, hobbies, interests and the way these people use their mental faculties.

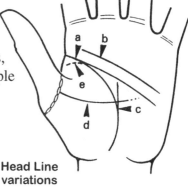

Head Line variations

Head Line Linked to the Life Line

The head and life lines often grow out of one line (a), and as long as they part fairly quickly on the hand, this is no bad thing. These people have a strong sense of family duty and they may not be in a hurry to leave home and become independent.

Head Line Tied to the Life Line

When these two lines are tied for a long stretch at the start, the owners have a strong sense of family duty and may also lack the courage to stride out on their own. They cling to the clan for support and can be very selective about friendships. This situation isn't always down to a fear of leaving the nest, because there might be a reason for the on-going family connection. For instance, there may be a handicapped or needy family member that the subject chooses to take care of, or at least be in regular contact with. Sometimes, an interfering parent wants to run the subject's life even after they are married with children of their own. In some cases, these people might marry and find themselves stuck with an unsavoury partner, or dragged into a dreadful in-law situation, where the spouse's parents, brothers or sisters are utterly horrid and try to control them.

When this formation is present, another scenario can exist, where the subject can't make a decision without talking things over with the family. This can result in them handing over too much power to a parent, a family member or even their partner. This is especially so if the partner is much older, richer or of a higher class and has a controlling nature.

Head Line Separate from Life Line
When there is a gap between the head line and the life line (b), the individual will be very independent. Palmistry theory suggests these people will leave home and go their own way early in life; while this can be so, it can also be the case that the person stays near the family unit, but has a mind of his own and therefore sees no need to escape. If the gap is extremely wide, then there will be a tendency not to look before leaping.

Head Line Starting on Jupiter
This person will be motivated and a good organiser. With a driven nature, he will get much done and will be a good and fair boss.

Sloping Head Line
In Vedic palmistry, this represents those who are on a spiritual quest. They will seek out all things esoteric and try to improve their lives and the lives of others around them. If the head line sinks too low on the hand, they can have day-dreamy natures and won't have a grasp on reality.

Straight Head Line
These owners are realistic but somewhat blinkered to any new ideas. They respect authority and like things done in a proper manner. In my experience, this type of person doesn't change his mind quickly and can be quite dogmatic.

Short Head Line
When the head line is short, these people don't strive too hard and can live mundane lives. They fear changes and challenges and prefer a regular routine to make them feel safe. As they are self-centred, they will talk endlessly about their hobbies, such as train spotting, golf, or gardening, and have no real interest in the conversation of others.

Their tempers are erratic and they are often unreasonable. If the line is red, they could have a violent streak and be prone to lash out in frustration. This is especially so if the line is short, straight and then dips down suddenly at the end.

Long Head Line
The owner will be driven, energetic and have a great mental aptitude. Their memory will be second to none and they usually enjoy great success. The direction of the head line must be taken into account. If the line travels straight across the palm, there could be successes in maths, science and business, but if it slopes, the subject might enjoy art, writing, spirituality, creativity, and so on.

Break in Head Line
This person will have to take care of accidents, especially if the lines are overlapping. If a square is on the formation and connects the lines, then all will be well.

Bitty, Broken Head Line
Sometimes this can represent poor areas of concentration and the individual can be forgetful. If the head line has too many broken lines, large islands and grilles, the person could suffer with mental problems and erratic mood swings. Sometimes when studying the female hand, you will see these formations when they are hormonal. Further up the line it can become settled again when the problem has subsided. Check if the Luna mount is red or mottled to verify this.

Trident on the end of Head Line
When this is in place, the owner will be gifted with writing and there will be a strong probability of published work. If there is just an ordinary fork, then the gift of writing will still be there, but this time perhaps for the person's own pleasure or, within an organization for commercial work, creating Power Point presentations and so on.

Chained Head Line
This can mean a predisposition towards cluster headaches for the individual who could also be plagued with tiredness and apathy. When the chains are small and run along the whole of the head line, the owner could have eye problems. Their sight might be good one day but blurry the next. If this was an on-going situation, recommend a visit to their doctor. If there is a largish island or a cluster of them below the area of

the Saturn mount and finger, the person may suffer deafness and if the same formation occurs below the Apollo mount and Apollo finger, there could be eye problems. If there are two large circles on the head line - and they have to be exactly round and red - then the person might suffer from glaucoma.

I remember reading the palm of a doctor many years ago and saw this formation on his hands. I asked if he had been suffering serious sight problems and then tentatively asked if he had seen an eye specialist. Bluntly he asked, "What are you trying to say, Beleta?" Gently I asked him if there was any glaucoma in his family. He replied abruptly "I had glaucoma diagnosed three months ago, is that what you are trying to tell me?"

This is a note from Sasha:

"Beleta amazed me when she came out with the comment about my fluctuating eyesight when she looked at my hands, because my sight does fluctuate. I have diabetes, and when there's too much sugar floating in my bloodstream, the lenses of one or both eyes become clouded. I sometimes suffer haemorrhages at the back of one or other of my eyes, which practically blinds me for a week or two at a time. Beleta told me that if the islands are pale, the eyesight will fluctuate, while if they are blue, red or standing out in some other way, the problem is likely to be permanent."

Islands on the Head Line

Islands are slightly different from chains as they are longer and less rounded; often they will be called 'slung loops chains' by a professional palmist. If they are seen on the palm, especially the head line, the owner will often feel trapped, perhaps in their marriage, relationship or job.

If the rest of the hand is aggressive and angry, or when the person has the murderer's thumb, they might have done a spell in prison. If the islands are at the start of the head line, the person might have had an unhappy childhood in school or home life. See also the Cat's Cradle formation.

Cat's Cradle and Triangles

The cat's cradle looks like the children's game with string or wool. The children would make intricate patterns, which they entwined around their fingers. If this type of formation commences at the start of the head line and life line, it is often an indication that the person disliked school, or less commonly, the subject may have liked school, but used it as an escape from an unhappy home life. A sharp island that looks like a triangle hanging on the line can indicated the person wasn't free to follow their dreams. We rarely see this configuration now, but it was a common sight among young men who had done National Service and hated the experience. These days we might link it to someone who's done a short spell in prison or community service through criminal or antisocial behaviour.

Twisted Wavy Head Line
These characters can be unstable and have a weak mentality. If they are addicted to drink or drugs, they can be unpredictable. They could even be bipolar.

Arched Head Line
These are tough, determined individuals who set out to get what they want and can be ruthless. Unconcerned about the feelings of others, they can crush anyone who gets in their way.

Upward Branches
These types listen to their heads rather than their hearts, and they are usually very successful in all they do because of their focused nature. If the branches drop down, then there could be a period of bad luck for the individual.

Crosses
Not a good omen as the owners will be prone to bad luck and upsets throughout their lives. These folk need to take great care to do everything properly as they can soon find themselves in a muddle through lack of forethought.

Purple Dots
If purple dots are present, the owner has to take great care of head injuries. If a square surrounds the dot, then protection will be given.

9: The Heart Line

The Heart Line

There can be controversy about where the heart line begins. Some traditional palmists say that it begins under the Mercury mount whilst the Vedic palmists say it begins under the Jupiter mount and as this is a book that inclines towards Vedic palmistry, we will take the latter pathway.

The heart line can reveal much about the owner's emotional state and it can also offer information about health. Sometimes my clients are anxious because their heart line is broken and short. Younger people think their marriages will be short-lived or unhappy when this is present on their hands, so when this happens I reassure them that there are many things on the palm that concern love and relationships and that one line cannot be taken in isolation, as it won't show the full picture.

Trident Fork at the Source on the Jupiter Mount

This is a really lovely thing to see as it represents a spiritual person who will help many in their lifetime due to their wonderful insight and inspiration. In Vedic palmistry, this mark can represent an "earth avatar type" who has come to earth to change the way people think. My grandmother linked this formation to clairvoyance and dream sleep premonitions.

Long Straight Heart Line

These individuals are loyal, loving and caring to their partners, families and friends, especially if the heart line is unbroken. The line should have a nice rosy tinge of pink.

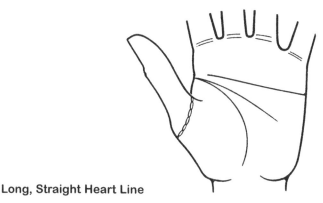

Long, Straight Heart Line

Short Heart Lines

I have found that short heart lines belong to very down-to-earth individual's of both sexes who can be single minded in their pursuit of love. If the heart line blends with the attachment lines, the person will want to have the upper hand in relationships and family matters. They can often be insecure and make themselves unpopular because of their out-dated Victorian principles. We see this type of heart line more often now, as many couples enter mixed marriages, so there can be issues if men from Eastern religions marry Western women who are used to a more independent lifestyle.

Weak and Fragmented Heart Line

One interpretation for this line is that these people can be unfaithful and inconsistent in love or friendships. As they are prone to change their minds, being in a relationship with them can be a bit of a roller-coaster ride. Where marriages are concerned they are usually doomed to failure. They may fall in love with people who are engaged or married to someone else. They could also go for the types that are into drugs or drink, and crime. I often call them "the victims". I have found they rarely value their friends, and pick them up and put them down at will. These individuals will drone on for hours about their problems, but will not be interested if their friends need a shoulder to cry on. As they set themselves up for failure before they start, friends and family will often have to bail them out and wait for them to grow up.

Islands on the Heart Line

The owner will be prone to deceit or affairs and can cause heartache within relationships. This can happen in reverse, where the subject is decent but their partner is not. Sasha and I agree with our friend Malcolm Wright, who says he has often found that an isolated island shows that a relationship has come to a sudden end, for example, a partner going out for a pint of milk and never returning. If the island is under the Apollo finger, there could be eye problems for the person.

Broken Heart Line

A break in an otherwise decent looking heart line can signify a broken heart. If the line starts up again and becomes strong, these subjects don't ever forget what has happened to them, but they do move on to live, love and be happy again.

Squares on the Heart Line

This can represent extreme tension for the individual and they could suffer from their nerves. As squares represent protection, they usually weather the storm and come out smiling. Another common scenario is that the person's emotional life is temporarily restricted. This can be because they feel alone, or they may be longing for love because they are in an unloving relationship.

Downward Branches

If there are quite a few of these, a series of disappointments and quarrels could occur for the person. These, however, are usually short-lived.

Upward Branches

This is a good thing to see on the heart line as it represents success, love, and new friendships that could be long lasting.

Circles on the Heart Line

This can mean the owner will have to take care with problems of the heart. If they are overweight this could be a serious matter. As I said earlier in the book, a palmist is not here to diagnose or frighten their clients, so caution is warranted when giving a reading.

Wavy Heart Line

This too can sometimes mean cardiac trouble or problems with the blood. It can also denote uncertainty with the person's focus in life.

Double Heart Line

This looks as though the subject has two heart lines. The second heart line can repair any defects of the original heart line, especially if the original is untidy and bitty. Its owner will be very devoted with old-fashioned principles.

Heart Line Running Right Across the Hand

This line will be very long and not often seen. It represents a person who is acutely sensitive and aware of everything that is going on in their environment. They will have high empathy with animals, world issues and mankind. Often life will make them feel depressed or hopeless because of their respect for the condition of all living things.

The Twig

When a short line sits horizontally on top of the heart line on the Saturn mount, this can represent divorce or separation. If there is another line on top of that, there could be more than one divorce for the person. If seen on a younger client's hand, be sure to tell them, "marry in haste, you'll repent at leisure". It would be better for them to wait for marriage until they reach the late twenties or early thirties to be sure of real happiness in love.

10: The Simian Line

The Simian Line

The Simian line (also known as *The Single Transverse Palmar Crease)* is formed when the head and heart lines fuse together into one crease, and it commences between the Jupiter finger and the thumb. Emotional and mental energies blend together to give the owner a struggle between thoughts and emotion. If seen on both hands, which can be quite rare, the owner could be highly creative, inventive and unique, especially with art or writing. If the line is only present on the non-dominant hand, its owner can have an erratic energy that could cause mayhem within their lives. If seen on only the dominant hand, the person could have an effect on others, perhaps in a disturbing or cathartic way. One thing for sure is that the lessons learned will help the soul to grow to a better understanding and awaken it to a deeper spiritual consciousness.

The name Simian comes from the word monkey or ape, because old-time palmists assumed that it was seen on some primates' palms.

There is much controversy and research on the Simian line, which causes huge differences of opinion in the world of palmistry. Some say there is a higher percentage of the Simian line formation seen in Down's Syndrome people or babies with prenatal rubella and leukaemia, and a host of other health problems have been mentioned in different books and articles. Others will argue that the Simian line is more abundant in certain cultures. There seems to be an agreement that there is a bigger percentage of this line in ethnic groups, and that it is more often seen in the male hand than the female.

Often a client will be horrified to be told they have this line and imagine all sorts of disturbing things, so reassurances have to be given and the bigger picture explained clearly to them. In modern day palmistry, we are inclined to be less critical of this formation. A Simian line owner can be highly intellectual, hold down a powerful job and inspire others with their determination and tenacity. A prime example is ex-Prime Minister Tony Blair, who has a Simian line on each hand.

Negative Traits

As they are prone to bossiness, they must take care not to upset others, and if they come into contact with another bossy person, then often the feathers will fly! Usually the line will only be present in one hand, but if it's in both, then it can be more dramatic, and palmistry can point to health problems with the heart. There is not much research to back this up, but it does seem to hold a lot of truth in my experience as a palmist. Simian line owners who have a gentle nature can sometimes be bullied, therefore they must stand up for their beliefs.

Meaning

A Simian line owner will be intense and highly focused, to the point of obsession; their drive and ambition will be second to none and they can achieve great things. Their personality is tense and hyperactive and they can be totally consumed with themselves, over-riding others who stand in their way. They will find it hard to separate emotions from thoughts and will hold deep secrets in their hearts. Many will be interested in religion. Others will want to deviate to a more liberal spiritual belief, but even so they will still live by tradition. When they are in power, their unwavering focus can get much done, but, because they can be so rigid, they are likely to upset others, and this can bring negativity in its wake.

On a plus point, they have a wicked sense of humour and can be great fun to be with; when times are good they become excited, happy and joyful.

In Love

Simian line owners are said to be secretive about their love life and don't often reveal their feelings for someone until they are very sure. As they don't like to be manipulated they can often go for a weaker type of partner who they can influence. In the bedroom there can still be some control, but once they are truly in love, the barriers should come down.

Their only fault is that they could neglect their loved ones for work, as their burning ambition will take precedence.

As a parent, they can be exacting and want the best for their children. They won't be a pushover either, as they will have strong principles and traditional ideas of discipline. Many parents are softened by their love for their children and will bend the rules for them, but a Simian line type can be less sentimental.

Semi- Simian Line

This formation has a very short, stick-like heart line. These owners do not blend well in society and are difficult to talk to, as they are neurotic and obsessive. Through recent years, I have seen more autistic or mentally challenged youngsters with this configuration. Often they will be obsessed with play-stations and computer games and take a long time to reach maturity. Sadly, this type will rarely be happy in love and can end up repressed and lonely.

11: The Fate Line

This important line has a wealth of information for the seeker. It will reveal a person's destiny, fortune and career, not to mention character. Some palmists, who also happen to be into astrology, link this line with Saturn. It often travels up the hand towards the Mount of Saturn, although it can go in a variety of directions.

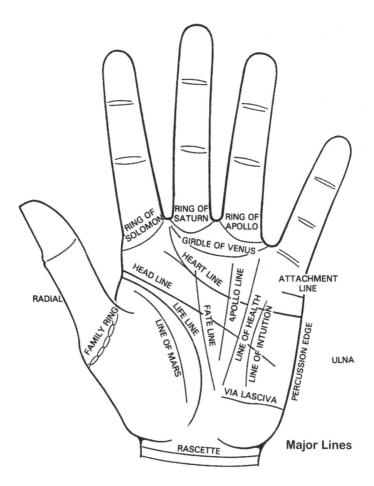

Major Lines

Rising from the Neptune Mount

When the fate line starts from the Neptune mount and ascends to the Saturn finger, these individuals will likely have a long life, and natural ending when life is done.

Rising from the First Rascette of Venus

If this ends below the Saturn finger then it portrays a good life with lashings of help from fate and destiny to help the owners on their way. These types succeed in all things and make a mark on the world.

Rising on the Lunar (or Moon) Mount

These people have moods that are very much affected by the moon and they have a psychic nature. Their lives are ruled by fate, which makes them winners at times, but they become badly blocked when they try to change their destiny in any way. This position is often found on the hands of white witches or people who follow the Wiccan belief. In Vedic palmistry this represents an old soul who has reincarnated to help others. Those who have fate lines that start on Luna will be valued by people far and wide, but not necessarily appreciated or understood within their own family.

Rising from the Life Line

When the fate line rises from the life line, the person will have to strive for their happiness and create their own success. As they don't always believe in destiny giving them a hand, they will work hard, and they will be envied and admired by those around them. If the line starts from the Mount of Venus, inside the life line, they may work in a family business, inherit money that will give them a good start in life, or have a very supportive and loving family around them.

A Long Strong Fate Line

Fate plays a big part in these people's lives, which will be eventful, especially if the line has a lot of disturbance on it. A very long line with little disturbance is found on the hands of those who find their way early in life and see things through with little change. They may also have a keen work ethic and a strong sense of duty.

Starting Late on the Hand
Many individuals have fate lines that don't start until half way up the palm or even higher. These types may drift along until fate throws something at them and then, belatedly, they make an effort in life.

Termination on the Mount of Jupiter
This is a sign of success, but it can be at the cost of the individuals' personal lives, possibly because they put more energy into their careers than into loving relationships.

Termination on the Mount of Saturn
If the line is neat and not tasselled, the owners will be well prepared for life and will be successful after a period of hard work.

Termination on the Head Line
This isn't a good sign, as these people are prone to being slapdash. They don't think ahead and so make many mistakes that others will have to rectify. I find this type take a long time to grow up and they blame others for their misfortunes. In Vedic palmistry such a person would be regarded as a young soul who hasn't reincarnated very often and would need the support of their family to instruct them in life skills, sometimes even into their forties.

Horizontal Lines
If there are many horizontal lines clearly indicated on the fate line, it can be a difficult or disturbing life for the owner. They could be plagued with ill luck and unhappiness. In Vedic palmistry this configuration can mean the owner is reincarnating to become a wiser soul by learning life's lessons the hard way.

Upward Branch
This is a fortunate line as it means the person will have a positive change. Their position will improve financially and they could enjoy a more exciting life. If the line branches downwards then the opposite could occur.

Triangle

When there is a triangle on the base of the fate line this could mean some sort of scandal will hit the person's life and cause mayhem for the individual and their family.

Island

When an island is present on the fate line, there will be a period of hardship. It can even represent the loss of a spouse. If a square surrounds the island the situation could be averted. If the line splits into a long island where two lines run parallel for a long way, the subject will suffer a sustained period of unhappiness. This can be self- induced. The main cause is they are hanging onto a situation or a person from their past.

One of Sasha's clients had a lengthy narrow island of this type and said her husband had left her, but it took her many years to come to terms with the fact. The poor woman had given up much of her life to longing, yearning and fighting hard for something that was never going to happen. What a waste of a precious life!

12: The Girdle of Venus

Girdle of Venus

The Girdle of Venus is a semi-circular line that sits high above the heart line and under the Apollo and Saturn fingers; it will be on or around the Apollo and Saturn mounts.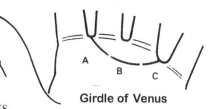

Girdle of Venus

Some people confuse this line with a double heart line so care must be taken to make the right diagnosis.

Not everyone has a Girdle of Venus, but many people have tasselled bits of one. New palmists sometimes link this line to sexuality and while it can relate somewhat to the libido, Vedic palmistry sees a strong Girdle of Venus as belonging to those who are driven and passionate about a project or particular aspect to their lives.

Traditional palmistry and Vedic palmistry disagree strongly with the formation of a perfectly formed Girdle of Venus. The traditional palmist sees a strong Girdle of Venus as a sign of weakness, signifying these subjects are emotionally destructive and can cause mayhem in their love lives. Traditionalists prefer to see a bitty and broken Girdle of Venus rather than a whole one, but Vedic palmistry takes the completely opposite view.

Fragmented Girdle of Venus

This person will not be as driven as those who have a complete Girdle of Venus, but they could have a talent for literary work. They are often inspired and highly sensitive and will love to mix with people who are like-minded. When I see this formation, which is rather like a wiry arc, I would encourage my client to join a writing circle.

Multiple Girdle of Venus

This formation has two or three (or more) strong, unbroken lines that sit directly under each other, and often the mounts will be red in colour. There are two distinct types of person here; one could be called the angel and the other a devil. If the lines are very red, then I would class the type of person as negative; if the lines are a delicate pink, the person will be positive.

The angelic types will have a compassionate nature and will devote their lives to spirituality and to the psychic sciences. They will understand the paranormal and be into clairvoyance, and perhaps palmistry, tarot, astrology and so forth. Many become experts in esoteric matters and go on to be teachers. I had a friend who used to be a brother of the White Eagle Lodge. In his life, he did much for children's charities abroad and had a deep faith about the afterlife. He is also a healer and a lover of the animal kingdom. The lines are very strong on his Girdle of Venus.

The diabolical type of person is preoccupied and obsessive about sex, and might have a stash of pornography or sexy DVDs to titillate the libido. These people may enhance their moods with stimulants, drugs, strip clubs and prostitutes, and some will become obsessive about on-line pornography sites.

Fragmented Multiples

If the double or triple lines on the Girdle of Venus are sketchy and broken, the owners can sometimes end up on the wrong side of the law.

13: Sibling Lines

There has sometimes been controversy in palmistry where the sibling lines are concerned. Some palmists pay them scant attention, whilst others will study then in great depth. In Vedic palmistry the lines are poured over and they can give current insight as to what is happening to the person's brothers or sisters.

The lines for the siblings are located on the radial side of the hand on the Jupiter Mount edge. If you fold your fingers toward you, you can usually see the lines quite clearly. If the lines are absent, one would assume you would be an only child. Count the number of horizontal lines and it should give an accurate picture of how many siblings there are. Traditional palmists will also refer to the lines to show close relationships, such as half siblings, cousins and very close friends.

Square on the Sibling Line
The owner's brother of sister might have to go through a difficult period in their lives, but will be protected and come out victorious.

Cross
If there is a cross on the sibling line, the person's brother or sister might be hurt in an accident, but if a square surrounds it, then there will be a positive outcome.

Star
The sibling has had a shock.

Grilles
When grilles are present the owner could have a long-running feud with his sibling and they could be estranged. Usually this would be emotional rather than linked to money.

Triangle
This is a good omen as the sibling could come into money and treat his kinfolk to cash to make their lives easier.

Vertical Lines
As a family there would have been great hardship for all of the siblings, but a close bond would be forged to form a united front.

Purple Dot
This can sometimes mean a sibling is very ill or have a short life span. Another aspect to this formation can be a sibling who might have died at birth or was a late miscarriage.

Extra Lines
If there are extra sibling lines that the subject does not know about on the hand, there might be a secret love child in the background that a parent might not have revealed to the family. A half sibling might have been adopted at birth, or there might have been an affair resulting in a baby that was hushed up. If there is an extra line this can indicate twins, but one of them may have been lost before, during or shortly after the birth.

14: The Quadrangle

(Also called The Angel's Landing Strip)

A Perfect Quadrangle

This should be evenly spaced at each end and at the central point. There should be no marks or blemishes within it other than the passage of the fate line and possibly the Apollo lines; the colour should be a medium pink. For true perfection there should be the Mystic Cross standing independently of head and heart line in the centre. This represents well-balanced individuals who are stable, loyal and friendly. Their tolerance levels are high and they will be good listeners with an uncanny knack of judging people correctly.

If the quadrangle is narrow, the person might be intolerant and fond of setting standards for others by being critical and possibly even sarcastic about them. They try to put others right, and can be very patronising and wearing to live with. If the quadrangle is wide, the subject isn't likely to pressurise or criticise others, but will leave them to do their own thing. If the head line falls away due to having a deep slope downwards, the person might be spiritual, poetic and rather soft-hearted.

Health

When the quadrangle is wide at each end but narrow in the centre, its owner will have trouble with the lungs, emphysema and sometimes asthma and chest infections. Heavy smokers can have this configuration and the central quadrangle can be red and enflamed.

If there are many lines, dashes and crosses in the quadrangle, the subject will be muddled and will have a difficult and problematic life.

Star Burst

If there is a star burst formation in the quadrangle, its owner will have the privilege of seeing something wonderful in their lives. It could be an angel, fairy, spirit, UFO or other paranormal phenomenon.

15: The Minor Lines

There are many minor lines on the hand, and not everyone will have all of them, because each of us is different. The minor lines can be confusing.

Travel Lines

This is an area of palmistry that comes directly from Vedic tradition and it was unknown in the West until about twenty-five years ago. Western palmists have now discovered that it works and have added it to their store of knowledge.

Travel lines appear on the percussion edge of the hand and they show up anywhere from under the Mount of Mercury, just under the heart line, downwards. Therefore, they appear on the percussion edge of the

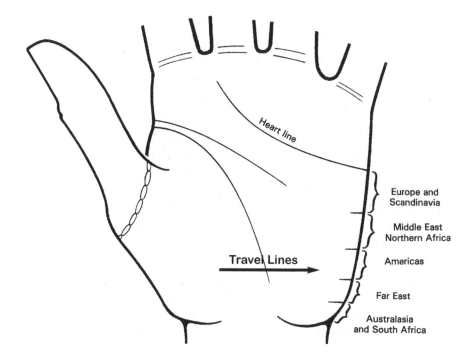

Heart line

Travel Lines

Europe and Scandinavia

Middle East Northern Africa

Americas

Far East

Australasia and South Africa

Mount of Mars and the Mount of the Moon. Look closely for horizontal lines in this area and carefully add up each line, because each one will represent a journey in the person's life.

The dominant hand holds future information and the non-dominant hand usually represents past information for journeys already taken. Some palmists believe if the non-dominant hand has many travel lines and the owner hasn't travelled, they will yearn to do so.

Where in the World?
Many years ago, Sasha realised these lines represented important journeys, and she soon found that she could tell which countries her clients had visited in the past or was due to visit in the future.

She discussed these findings with an Indian colleague who used the Vedic tradition, and his response amazed her. He rummaged around in his papers and handed her a photocopy of a hand with many fine lines drawn in on the percussion edge, each one marked with the name of a country. The information was much more detailed than the work she had done, but tallied with her own diagnosis.

Cross on a Line
This doesn't bode well, because the person might have a journey that is perilous in some way. If a square is encompassing the cross then the disaster will be averted. Crosses can sometimes represent accidents or broken bones.

One Chain on the Line
An emotional upset which could spoil the journey, so there might be an argument with a travelling companion. My daughter Leanna has this formation and this is how it played out in her life. When she was just seventeen she went on holiday to America with a female friend. When her friend met a would-be lover, she chased after him to a different state, leaving my daughter for over a week, very distressed at being left alone in a strange country.

Loop Chains
Loop chains on a travel line suggest a difficult journey with many obstacles. Suitcases could go missing and accommodation might be disappointing. It can represent one upset after another and the feeling that you need another holiday to recover from the one you have just

had! I have this formation on my hand and whilst in Canada my suitcases were lost for five days. All I had on me were the clothes on my back and my handbag!

Vertical Lines

Thin red vertical lines on a travel line can represent illness whilst abroad so the individual can return home with a virus or an upset stomach. If a cross is present on the line, the traveller could spend some time in hospital.

Pentagram

If a pentagram appears on a line of travel, the owner will be really blessed with a stunning holiday or a mind-blowing experience. They may swim with dolphins or perhaps see the Aurora Borealis, or go trekking in the Amazon Forest.

Three Horizontal Lines

When three lines are linked together, the subject will visit three different locations or perhaps three islands on one visit. This is seen more often due to cruises or coach tours.

A Purple Dot

A purple dot is not a good thing to see on a travel line as it represents great anxiety or a shock. To be fair, this sign is not often seen on the hand, but you can bet your life the person has undergone or will undergo, some terrible ordeal, such as an attack or a robbery or suddenly finding themselves lost and off the beaten track. My nephew has this formation and when he was in Thailand, he was badly bitten by a starving dog. He loves dogs so he was really upset and shocked by the incident for many months.

A Fork

A fork can mean the person will have to make a detour on their journey. I have this mark on my palm, and many years ago the plane I was travelling in had air conditioning problems and we were relocated to another airport until the problem was fixed.

A Half Triangle

When this sign is on a travel line, it is a good omen. Money or riches can be made in a foreign country. If the life line has a fork on it as well, the person might decide to work and live abroad and will enjoy an opulent life style there.

The Via Lasciva

This line used to be called the poison line, or the allergy line. When studied closely, it can give a good diagnosis of the person's health, and it can also be linked to travel. It is not present on everyone's hand.

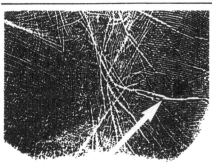

The Via Lasciva

Broken Via Lasciva

If the Via Lasciva is broken or bitty and has an island or two present, the owners will struggle with their diet and food intake. They might starve for a week and then binge on all the wrong types of food. Some subjects could have a drink problem, and this can be seen if the line is red and blotchy.

Long, Clear Via Lasciva

This can represent sensitivity to chemicals and medicines, plus allergies to foods such as peanuts, wheat, etc. I have found that with this type of line, the person is into alternative medicines and systems such as healing, homeopathy and herbal remedies, and will have success in maintaining a healthy lifestyle. The owner may be gifted with healing for others.

The Mars Line

The line of Mars lies between the line of life and the thumb and it ends on the Mount of Venus. Push the thumb towards the Jupiter finger and look for a short line on the inside of the life line. Inexperienced palmists can confuse this with another line which is the sister life line or the inner life line, which also sits quite close to the life line, but the line of Mars is a good quarter of an inch away from it. When found, this is classed as very lucky. When seen on both hands this is really special and if the line is long then the person should have a charmed life.

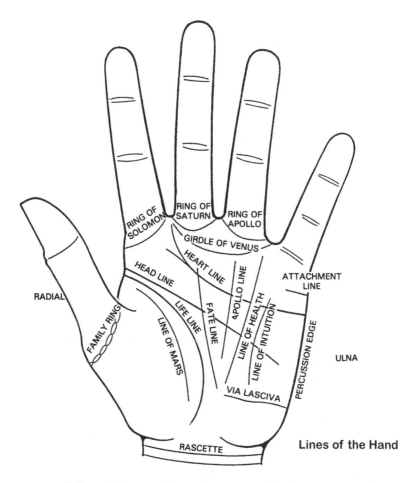

Lines of the Hand

A strong Mars line will represent vitality, strength and determination. Often this line will be seen in people who are connected to the forces and occupations that require bravery such as the fire and rescue services and some types of sport. The owner will be talented in a special way and will often shine in their particular field. In years gone by, this line often showed up on those who were conscripted into the National Service and who thoroughly enjoyed the experience. Now you may find it on the hands of people who enjoyed their time as scouts, guides and cadets. In short these types enjoy being away from home, being a part of a team and facing challenges. The owner of a strong Mars line will be blessed with a good constitution and if they do become ill, will get better very quickly.

Fragmented Mars Line
In Vedic palmistry, a broken and fragile line of Mars can denote stomach and digestive disorders. If the line is tasselled or chained then the person could be prone to headaches.

Sister Life Line or Shadow Life Line
You sometimes see a second line that lies close to the life line; this gives strength to the life line, so it helps the individual recover from illness or setbacks in life. It can be an indication that members of the subject's family who have died are looking after them, from the "other side".

Apollo Line – Also Known as the Sun Line
The Apollo line runs up the hand from the wrist end to the finger end, in a similar way to the fate line, but located towards the ulna side of the fate line. It usually commences near the wrist and ascends vertically to the Apollo finger.

This is a brilliant aspect to see as it brings wealth, health and happiness and it is said the person should have an idyllic life with many blessings and fame. Needless to say, palmists don't often see a perfect Apollo line. In Vedic palmistry, the owner will have endured many hard past lives, so this time round, they reap the blessings of their past trials and tribulations.

The origins of the Apollo line can vary a great deal and can be confusing, but in time you should get a feel for the procedure. I usually scan the Apollo mount, as there's often something there to help.

Apollo Line Starting Inside the Life Line
This is an unusual formation. It shows the owner will have received lots of help from their family early on, which has helped them succeed in life. The owner will enjoy art and books and will have a keen intellect. This subject can weigh up others in an instant.

Mount of the Moon
When this line ascends from the Moon mount to the Apollo finger, the owner will be gifted in all things pertaining to the arts. This could be writing, acting, dancing or singing. They will inspire those around them and will have a double dose of charisma and definitely have the X Factor!

Apollo Line on the Plain of Mars
This is easily confused with the fate line and can often be seen running side by side with it. These people will eventually reach their goals, but only with a great deal of personal struggle and determination. They are proud and independent.

Apollo Line Emerging from the Fate Line
Those who have hands that show an Apollo line connecting half way up the hand will succeed in the arts. These subjects will have strokes of good luck that help them on their journey. If they change tack and go after a completely different type of career later in life, that will also be successful.

Apollo Line Ending on the Heart Line
Although the owner will be driven to succeed, their emotional immaturity will hold them back. There will be wasted talent and lost opportunities and this type will often have excuses for their lack of success and will constantly blame others.

Apollo Line Ending on the Head Line
This is not a wonderful placement, because the owner will have real struggles in life through their lack of judgement. They find it hard to change their opinions and listen to reason. As far as finances are concerned, it could be bad news with bankruptcy on the agenda.

Apollo Line on the Apollo Mount
Even if this is the only part of the Apollo Line in evidence, the news is good, as it points to happiness in later life and an enjoyable old age.

The Mercury Line, also Known as the Hepatic Line
We look at this line to give an indication of the person's health and stamina, because the stronger the line, the stronger the person is. A thin broken Mercury line signifies a weak constitution. If you want to know if your client is stressed, a broken bitty line is a good indicator that they are under pressure and need to chill out.

The Medical Striata
The Medical Striata is the name of a small group of lines located on the Mercury Mount just above the heart line. There are often three little lines that rise up in a slightly diagonal direction, often with another line

crossing them in a slanting direction. However there can be as many as seven vertical lines. These marks show a very special gift and can be seen in the palms of spiritual healers, homeopaths and those practising complimentary medicines. They are also present on the hands of nurses, midwives, vets, doctors and dentists. I have a friend who is a psychologist, and she has these marks very clearly on her hand.

When looking at younger people's hands, the Striata can indicate that they will go into a life of medical service, and Vedic palmistry suggests that the child is gifted, with many blessings. It can also represent a wiser soul reincarnating to ease the burdens of others.

As the left hand is what destiny gives you and the right hand what you do with it, both hands must be looked at closely. If the medical striata are in the left hand but not the right, the person has blocked the gift in some way, and it can be a palmist's duty to remind them of their gift.

Moles, Warts and Blemishes

When looking at palms, you will sometimes see warts and skin eruptions, and these can give away mysterious secrets.

Warts are classed as a blockage, and the owner will have to work through the things in the area of that block. For example, if there is a large mole on the Mount of Venus, the person will be prone to making huge mistakes in love.

Temporary red patches show a shock, an illness, a worry or some other problem that has arisen around the time of the reading. The redness will go once the problem passes.

16: The Fingers

The Fingers Generally

Fingers that are quite long in proportion to the palm denote intellectual ability and mental power. When short and stubby looking, the subject is inclined to hold back, and may take longer to absorb and learn things; having said that, there are plenty of classical and modern musicians, composers and writers who have fingers shorter than their palms. They have fire hands, and as such are creative individuals.

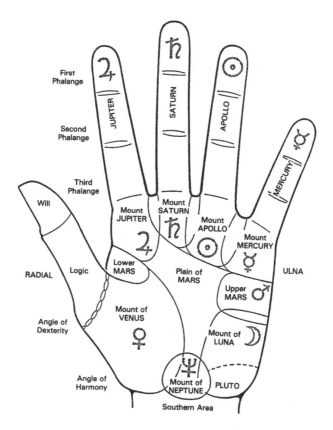

Bear in mind that the way the fingers are set on the hand can make them appear short, so use a ruler when comparing one finger with another.

» The index finger is called the finger of Jupiter.
» The middle finger is called the finger of Saturn.
» The ring finger is called the finger of the Sun or Apollo
» The little finger is called the finger of Mercury.

Jupiter Finger
The finger of Jupiter represents social consciousness, idealism and careers. When long, it means the owner could be in business for themselves and in charge of their own company or even a chain of companies. If short, it denotes a lack of confidence, a dislike of responsibility and no ambition. The person will prefer to melt into the background. When the finger is medium in length, then we will see a balanced individual.

Saturn Finger
The finger of Saturn represents trends, psychology and is sometimes called the finger of destiny. When long, it can mean prudence, a love of solitude and reserve. These people need peace and quiet and will love to study. When the Saturn finger is short, it denotes careless frivolity and a lack of seriousness in the person's life. Subjects with medium length Saturn fingers are balanced in all things.

Sun Finger or Apollo Finger
When long, it gives the owner a love of beauty and the desire for celebrity status and fame. The owner will like the arts, music, antiques, museums and ancient castles. They also love children and delight in helping them to grow through teaching. When excessively long, the ego will be large and the owner will like notoriety and will take risks when speculating. They will love money and perhaps gambling. Recent medical research shows a long Apollo finger owner will have a talent for engineering, technical drawing and computer software design. These folk can also be extremely clever with dress design and manufacture.

The Mercury Finger
If long, it represents mental power, eloquence and a grasp of languages and a fondness for scientific studies. The subject will be a great communicator

and lecturer. When short, it denotes a difficulty in the spoken word and in the expression of thoughts. When crooked or in-turned, secrecy will be present in their nature. A pointed Mercury finger can denote a psychic ability especially if the other fingers are not pointed.

17: Inclination

The way the fingers lean is interesting, and this is something you can even spot at a distance without the person being aware of your interest.

Restricted - No Gaps between Fingers

People who have this kind of hand often appear very outgoing, but this is in contrast to their true nature. Indeed some are wonderful sales people and others are politicians or very public figures, but they are not what they seem. These subjects are extremely private and introverted. They may have lacked attention in their childhood, which has left them feeling insecure. They need to feel completely in control of their lives. Their love relationships can be strained because they are possessive, due to their fear that their partner might stray. Politicians with hands that don't allow any light to shine through the fingers won't want to listen to the opinions of others. Cash wise, these folk can be tight fisted. They will make sure they have everything they want, but will deny others any luxuries.

Inwardly Inclining Fingers

This is an unusual formation, and one that will not often be seen. There are two possibilities here: the first is that these people are very interesting, but hard to read for, because they are secretive and on their guard. These individuals trust no one and prefer others to fight their battles for them. Often they will feel the grass is greener on the other side of the hill.

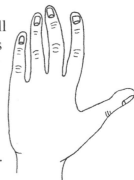

They need to get pleasure from making money from their crafts or hobbies.

The second possibility is their having some kind of mental handicap, perhaps including Down's syndrome.

Space between Jupiter and Saturn

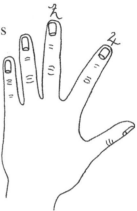

These people will always follow the dictates of their hearts. They will be good workers and often have their own business in which they succeed, but they are not clever when it comes to personal relationships. This may be due to a selfish streak. Success is more important than love.

Saturn and Apollo Leaning
Towards Each Other

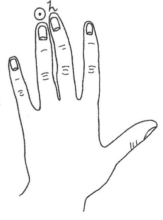

This is quite a common arrangement. These subjects will need a lot of understanding and security, because they have fragile egos. They must also have job satisfaction, which they will prefer to lots of money.

Saturn and Apollo Leaning Away From Each Other

These people are rather lonely and they daydream about the past. When they are down, they can be rebellious and difficult at home or work. They find it hard to face the future or plan ahead, and hate being the centre of attention, because of their shyness. Once they are settled and happy, with family and good friendships, their natural sense of humour and goodwill shines through.

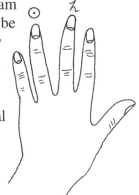

Space between Apollo and Mercury

This is a common sight, although the spacing can vary from a small gap to a very large one.

These people are very intuitive and can sometimes read the minds of others. Inwardly, they are quite lonely and like their own space. If they don't have space, they could feel suffocated and nervous. In relationships, their partner must understand their need for independence and freedom. They won't rush into new relationships, as they are cautious about love. This hand type makes an excellent parent. Until they really trust someone, they are not easily influenced. They prefer straight-talking people.

Mercury Bent Inwards

Traditional palmists considered this a negative sign, with the owner being judged as manipulative, dishonest and secretive, especially where money matters are concerned. Some modern palmists look on this in a very different way, seeing the owner as the soul of discretion who will never divulge the secrets of others. This being the case, they can make excellent counsellors. As there is controversy about this formation, it is up to the individual palmist to decide, depending on the severity of the incline.

18: Fingertips

Spatulate Fingertips

Spatulate or splayed fingertips have an alien look about them and represent an active type of person who loves to be in the thick of things. In spite of this, these people crave open spaces. They are restless souls who are easily bored. Their minds are scientific and energetic. Often these people are inventive and ahead of their time, especially if they have the astrological sign of Aquarius.

Careers

These types would be happy as explorers, inventors, scientists, architects, barristers, industrial engineers or members the armed forces and emergency services. They like electronics.

In Love

To be totally happy in a relationship, these individuals must be allowed freedom. Partners must understand their wish to travel and explore. Their inventive minds are always seeking new thrills. They don't like to stay at home to raise a family, and will hate to be trapped a mundane job. For the marriage to survive with this type, it would be best to have exactly the same interests.

Health

These individuals suffer from nervous tension and muscle strain.

Rounded Fingertips

These people will put up with things for a long time, because they don't like to say no. Their souls are pure and hate to see ugliness or discord. In the home, they will be fussy about their ornaments and colour schemes. They have such a sweet disposition that they can be inclined to believe everything they hear, and they are far too trusting. Once they have been let down, they are cautious and find it hard to forgive.

Careers

Careers might include artists, interior designers, teachers, writers and dress designers. They are very good at figurework and bookkeeping.

In Love

These individuals are madly romantic and won't want to be alone. They like quiet evenings in with a good bottle of wine and a DVD. They remain faithful in love and are excellent parents.

Health

As this type hates any sort of confrontation, they will often suffer with their nerves and have to take care with insomnia.

Square Fingertips

These no nonsense types get straight to the point, so you will always know where you stand. They like routine, have their feet firmly planted on the ground and will put in a good day's work for a good day's pay. They don't mind long hours and will be punctual and conscientious, and make fair minded bosses. One thing is for sure, we need this type, as they make the wheels go around and see things get done properly.

Careers

They can make good bankers, accountants, lawyers, business people, teachers, cooks, and teachers.

Male in Love
This man is very fair and will respond to a clean house, meals that are produced on time, and fresh laundry in the drawer. For this, he will work hard and provide for his family. He may be a little Victorian in his outlook, but his love is long lasting and he will have old-fashioned manners. He won't forget birthdays and anniversaries, and he will be generous and tender, especially if he has an earth sign such as, Taurus, Capricorn or Virgo.

Female in Love
She will be a homemaker and adore children, especially as she has endless patience. The home will be spotless and run like clockwork, with home-cooked food on the table. She will have a strong traditional streak where her clan will take precedence.

Health
Usually this type has a robust constitution and will enjoy a long and healthy life. However, poring over documents and spending long hours in front of the computer might result in eye problems.

Conic Fingertips
This is a blend of rounded and pointed fingers. The owners will be quick-minded and alert, literally missing nothing, and with their shrewd nature, will be able to see through others in a nanosecond. Their sensitivity is second to none and they will often be psychic, especially if they have Scorpio strongly emphasised in their charts. Their temperamental nature can be off-putting, as they change from day to day. Sometimes they lack stamina and will really love their creature comforts, especially if the base pads are plump. The conic type will be very kind to animals.

Career
These types could be musicians, yoga teachers, clairvoyants and veterinary workers.

In Love
Conic types are a little lazy in love, but never boring. Their partners won't know with whom they are going to wake up each morning, because of their multifaceted personalities. What was said yesterday won't mean a thing today, so life will be a merry go round. If their

partner should stray, then you will see the sparks fly, as these subjects have mercurial tempers and a quick, spiteful tongue. On the positive side, they are great fun and often laugh their partners into bed. Sometimes they will love animals more than people.

Health
Conic owners can be prone to nervousness and digestive disorders. If the Jupiter phalanges are plump, over indulgence can be a problem.

Pointed Fingertips

These people are often glamorous and artistic, with a flair for fashion. You can find them rummaging around in charity shops and car boot sales looking for something different, and they love a bargain! I have often found with this type that they are inclined to be self possessed and critical of others. They will tell you what needs doing, but will they actually get off their backsides and do it themselves? If crossed, they never forget or forgive.

Career
These people can be fundraisers, fashion sales people, hairdressers and beauticians.

In Love
These types are dreamers. To them, the chase is usually better than the real thing. They enjoy being wined and dined, but once the passion has worn off, they look around for another romantic challenge. They need a strong partner who will take a no-nonsense approach with them. As parents, they will inspire their young and lavish time on them.

Health
These individuals lack stamina and get tired quickly, so they should take power naps to restore their energy.

Mixed Fingertips
People with mixed fingertips can have more than one career in their lifetime. They may have worked for years in the building trade and end up being a vet or a lay preacher. These types will never be boring, as they will have a go at anything, and their hobbies will be just as diverse. They will enjoy sport, painting, singing and so on.

Careers
Anything!

In Love
These people are flirtatious, as they love variety. They are good in bed and will experiment with enthusiasm. I find with this type that they never stay in one marriage, because they can be easily tempted. As parents, they will be good fun and will involve the children in all sorts of hobbies.

Health
These types are usually robust and their minds stay forever young.

Droplet Fingertips
This formation isn't often seen on a person's hand. The pads of the fingers are slightly bulbous and fleshy. It's best to slightly curl the fingers and raise the hand to eye level to see the effect to its best effect.

The person that has this type of finger tip will be very shrewd and will strive for perfection. Anything out of place will annoy these folks. They are artistic and extremely psychic. They are acutely aware of any atmospheres and will be difficult to fool. Some might say they have a cynical nature, but my belief is they can see ahead and strip away any preconceived ideas that others might have.

Careers
These individuals might take up tarot, Mediumship or counselling. Their love of art and creativity means they might pursue a career in fashion. They can make good beauticians, hair stylists, interior designers and masseurs. They are often excellent dressmakers, knitters or craft workers, with a wonderful sense of touch. As their touch is so sensitive, they might be drawn to things as diverse as fine carpentry, decorative cake-craft or dress design.

In Love
These people are hard to please, since they can more or less read their partner's mind. They have very high standards, so they won't waste time on endless affairs, but would prefer to wait for a soulmate to come along.

19: Fingerprints

The study of skin-ridge patterns, or fingerprints, is called Dermatoglyphics. This word is derived from derma, meaning skin, and glyph, meaning carving or design. There are five different types of fingerprint.

Fingerprints

Every person has a unique set of fingerprints, and fingerprints have a long history of being used as a form of identification. The ancient Babylonians often used fingerprints on clay tablets as a signature for their business transactions, and the ancient Chinese used thumbprints on clay seals. The human fingerprint is fully formed inside the womb at around sixteen weeks, and it's composed of between fifty and a hundred lines.

The use of fingerprinting by the police as a way of identifying criminals started in 1903 in the USA, and since then the method has been used all over the world.

Fingerprint Patterns

Whorls - Fire Element

Whorl on Jupiter
These people will be artistic and independent and strive to run their own businesses. They are very shrewd and nothing gets past them. As youngsters, they lack the carefree attitudes of their peer group, because they can see through situations and are wise beyond their years. They often put their own parents under the microscope.

Whorl on Saturn
If they respect someone, these folk will listen to and even motivate them into trying new things. They are nosy and love to get to the bottom of secrets and subterfuge. They have brilliant organisational skills and do everything to perfection.

Whorl on Apollo
These folk have moods that can swing from high to low within a few hours and they can be irritated if things are not just so. They hate untidiness and ugliness of any kind, and if they are partnered with a lazy mate, the marriage will seldom work.

Whorl on Mercury
Often people with this fingerprint will be quiet, retiring and self-conscious, and will need motivating, but once they get started on their given subject, they can rattle on for hours. They have an eagle eye, and will soon spot if something isn't right. Where spiritual faith is concerned, they will look into a variety of beliefs.

Whorl on Venus (the thumb)
Stomach or digestive disorders can be a problem for this type. They will have strong leadership gifts and love to be in charge. Usually they will make a good job of things because of their wonderful organisational skills. As a parent, they need to be less authoritarian and more easy-going.

Arches - Earth element
These are down-to-earth types who are the salt of the earth, very trustworthy and with good common sense. They will not believe anything unless they actually have proof. If the arches are on all fingers, this might indicate chromosomal abnormalities. On the negative side, they tend to have low self-esteem.

Arch on Jupiter
This type of fingerprint on Jupiter will bring frustration, and the owner will be inclined to bottle things up. They also

suffer with self-esteem issues. They save their money and will make sure there is a good investment plan for their future.

Arch on Saturn
The owner of this fingerprint will want to study, pass exams and gain knowledge. They are traditionalists, so they value older friends and take time to accept new ideas. They try to manipulate others.

Arch on Apollo
These types keep their feelings hidden, maintaining the British 'stiff upper lip.' They hate others to be over emotional and will often push things from their past into the deepest recesses of their mind.

Arch on Mercury
They enjoy tradition; they will not seek to change or rethink their own ideas, and so they become behind the times.

Arch on Venus – the Thumb
The owner will be practical and honest; what you see is what you get. This person will definitely have a domineering streak. They are passionate, but they can be blind to the faults of those whom they love.

Tented Arches - Air element

This is a formation with an upright central core. It is usually found on the Jupiter finger. People with this fingerprint can be highly-strung and sensitive and will strive to seek the truth in all matters. They usually have a hyperactive and fiery nature. It is rare to see the formation on all fingers, but if so, the person will love music and artistic projects.

Loops - Water element

This is the most common variety of fingerprint. Loop formations can come in from either side of the finger, although those that come from the thumb or radial side of the finger are less common than the ulna loops. Radial loops mainly appear on the Jupiter finger, but they can turn up on other fingers. Subjects with radial loops have stronger personalities than those with ulna loops. When on Jupiter, they have leadership qualities, will be bossy and want their own way. Ulna loop people are flexible, sociable and reasonable.

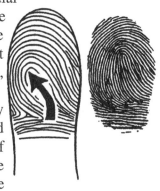

The owner of any loop print has many irons in the fire. Their gift is to be unique and they will often have ideas that are ahead of their time. They prefer to let others lead. If the loops are present on all fingers, then the individual will be very well balanced.

Loop on Jupiter
These people have good potential to be self-employed and successful in their chosen career.

Loop on Saturn
This type is usually inventive with a strong creative streak. They can make something out of nothing and, because of their unique approach, they will always be ahead of the game.

Loop on Apollo
This subject will be hard to understand and will spend much time on self-analysis. Unless this person has lived through a certain problem, he will not be able to empathise with the emotions of others. The old expression comes to mind, that you cannot teach what you haven't learned.

Loop on Mercury
This is a rare formation, and the person that has it will have radical views on religion and all things spiritual. Their concepts are modern and visionary and they seem to be able instinctively to know the truth. If you believe in reincarnation, this person would be classed as an old soul.

Double Loop
This person can see both sides of the story and can be a good mediator. They contemplate long and hard before making a decision. This print is usually found on the Jupiter finger or the thumb (Venus). The person is practical and into the material world, and can be a little inflexible.

When the double loop is small and tight, the person will be intuitive, but the intuition will confuse them, as they try to use logic instead of their gut feeling.

Peacock's Eye

This is a rare fingerprint. Its owner will be a perfectionist with an excellent eye for detail. In Vedic palmistry, this was also known as a sign of a magic person or a visionary. If it appears on the Apollo finger, the owner will be gifted in the arts and if on the Saturn finger, the person will be creative in things like carpentry, metalwork, engineering or sculpture. A Peacock's Eye on the mercury finger signifies an excellent writer or teacher.

20: Fingernails

Fingernails are made of a protein called keratin. If the nail is damaged or torn off completely, it will take between six and eight months to grow back. Hippocrates remarked that the nail reflects the condition of the body. We can find out a great deal about a person's character from the nail shape. The first things a good palmist will want to study are the fingernails, because there is a wealth of information displayed on them, especially concerning health. The texture, colour and shape of the nail must be taken into careful consideration.

Hard or Soft Nails
Nails tend to harden with age, and as many older people have discovered, toenails can become very difficult to cut in later life. However, those with hard nails are usually careful with money. They may or may not earn good money, but they tend not to overspend.

Soft nails can denote poor health, but also a self-indulgent nature, or just that the individual is in a phase of overspending. If your nails are normally all right but suddenly start flaking or becoming soft, examine your health and your bank balance!

Nail Shapes
The nail generally has one of five shapes: broad, oval, short, square and narrow. Healthy nails will be a pale pink colour with a decent moon at the bed of the nail and a slight bloom or sheen on them.

Broad Square Nails
People with broad, square nails have stamina and drive and will enjoy good health. Their faults are stubbornness and a need to be in charge. These folk have boundless energy and optimism, and usually succeed in all they do. They tend to not sit still, and their restless nature can sometimes be annoying to gentler souls.

They are prone to small and silly accidents. They might also suffer with tension to the shoulders and neck.

Narrow Nails
The owners of these nails have little stamina and a nervous temperament. Their spirit will lack courage and they could be apprehensive about even the smallest problems. One of their main faults is that they don't finish what they have started. They suffer from low self-esteem. These shaped nails can be found on people who suffer from fatigue.

Almond or Oblong Nails
These are lovely nails to have, as these subjects will have a sweet disposition. They do all in their power to help others in distress. They also love animals. Their nature is not to be confrontational, but to placate and help others in life.

They have a healthy constitution, but they could have a tendency to food allergies when older. Diabetes is a possibility here, too.

Fan Shaped Nails
The owners of these shaped nails have a nervous disposition and their energy and drive can be used up quickly. Even as children, they will like to sleep a lot, or have day-dreamy natures.

If very fan shaped and if the nails are red, these individuals can have psychological disorders. Another possibility is an addictive personality, so alcohol or drugs may be a problem at some point in their lives.

Watch Glass or Hippocratic Nails
These nails look like the glass cover of an old-fashioned pocket watch, as they are convex, sometimes even lifting from the beds at the sides. This person is mild mannered, easy to get along with and makes a fair and easy-going boss in the workplace.

Their owners have a tendency toward respiratory problems, and in days gone by, this was a classic formation for those with tuberculosis. If this formation is present in people who smoke, there is an elevated risk of an early death, often as a result of lung cancer. Asthma can be another condition, as can cirrhosis of the liver, sarcoidosis, emphysema and chronic bronchitis.

Sasha once told me a story about nails like these. She was sitting in a bookshop doing short readings in order to promote her own palmistry book, when a young woman who was the picture of health sat down opposite her. The moment Sasha saw her hands, she noticed the woman's watchglass nails. Sasha commented that a half-century ago, those nails would immediately alert a doctor that the patient had tuberculosis. The young lady answered she had recently spent several weeks in a special hospital, after catching TB while travelling in India!

Long Nails

This doesn't refer to people who happen to have grown their nails long; it's the length of the nail that's still on the nail bed.

These types have good imaginations, but if the nail is too long, they can live in a world of their own. Often these people will be interested in computer games and similar hobbies, and prefer to be engrossed in such pursuits rather than interact with others. The overall personality is pleasant, but they can lack drive and ambition, as they take everything at a leisurely pace. They lack vigour and could suffer with their backs and upper torso.

Small Nails

Those who have small child-like nails are exacting and shrewd, especially when female. They will love things to be in order and want everything spick and span. Unfortunately, they have a critical nature and can nag or nitpick, and they will never forget if they have been wronged. Their wit is sharp and they may delight in making their opinions known. They do have good common sense though, and will assess situations very quickly.

As they can be highly strung, their nerves may be a problem, and lack of sleep can make them irritable. Rest is important, even taking small catnaps if necessary.

Fingernail Colour

This can give information about the character of a person, their vigour - or lack of it - and their current state of health.

Medium Pink

This is the best colour to have. It shows quick mental appreciation and an affectionate nature. These individuals are well balanced and friendly.

Reddish

The people with this colour will have a strong sex drive and be highly tactile, but could have intense bouts of anger and high blood pressure. Their tolerance levels are low and they are constantly seeking new thrills.

Blue Tinge

Often these individuals will have poor circulation and feel the cold, so they are better suited to warmer climes. Their nature is slightly standoffish and they can be cold in love because they hide their feelings, therefore making it hard for their partners to understand them.

Yellow Tinge

The owners of this type of nail may have problems with their liver. They should drink plenty of water and keep their alcohol intake low. They are not great sleepers and can wake up intermittently through the night, so they are often tired.

Whitish Grey

This can be an indication of circulatory problems and often the hands will feel cold and clammy to the touch. These people can also suffer with pains in their joints, shoulders and back when older.

Opaque Nails

White opaque nails with a dark banding at the top of the nail can often depict diabetes.

The Moons

The moons are a crescent shaped formation that is a visible part of the nail matrix, and they have much to say about the client's constitution. Strangely, the moons are often absent on the Apollo finger, but they are almost always present on the thumb.

Normal Moons

A normal moon is a pale pink arc on the base of all the fingernails and this signifies good blood pressure and circulation. The owner will be even-tempered and easy to get along with.

Blue Moons

When the moons have a blue line hugging them, this will signify bad circulation and sometimes chilblains.

No Moons

This can be a sign of blood pressure and circulatory problems. If there is no moon on the Mercury fingernail the owner could suffer from lower back conditions, possibly as the result of an accident. If the moon is absent on the Apollo finger, creaky knees and joints could be a problem.

Over Large Moons

This can be indicative of an overactive heart and an excitable temper. This owner will not take stress very well and can live on adrenalin. They are not easy to live with, as their standards are sometimes unattainable.

Changing Moons

If the moons suddenly change by enlarging or disappearing, then this can represent heart problems.

Blue/Grey Arc on Moons

Sometimes there may be a bluish or grey arc sitting on top of the moon and the fingers feel cold or clammy. This is another sign of poor circulation. It seems to be more common in people who have the astrological sign of Aquarius.

Absent Moon on the Mercury Fingernail

This is quite common to see and the owners of this formation will usually suffer with lower back problems such as a slipped disc, usually caused by an accident when they were younger.

Fingernails and Health

When looking at the nails for health, it is important to stress that you must not frighten your clients when faced with the possibility of potentially serious problems. In my thirty years as a palmist, I have helped quite a few people to address their health issues, some of which they have known about, and some not. I have even saved lives. Only experience can teach the techniques of reading palms, and the first thing to learn is that you must be very careful about what you say, especially if you are at all unsure about the matter at hand… better to stay silent than to speculate.

However, if you feel sure, first gently ask the client if they have seen a doctor recently. If their answer is no, then you must decide whether to impart any information. This is the time that prior professional training in consulting and handling people shows its real need. It is not enough to cross fingers and hope that the client is an understanding type; you have as much responsibility as any doctor to your client, and if you presume to impart seriously disturbing information, you should be fully capable of handling any outcome. This skill does not come automatically, it has to be learned. Please speak in a calm, positive and reassuring way, and perhaps suggest they go to see their doctor for a general checkup.

Fluted or Beaded Nails
Fluted nails can be a sign of rheumatoid arthritis, rheumatic disorders and skin conditions such as eczema and acne. These tend to be seen on older hands, where the nail is often thickened and whitish in places.

Spoon Shaped Nails
When we see this on the fingernail, we know that the person is either suffering from a lack of nutrition, or may have had some recent trauma. This formation can also indicate an underactive thyroid. In more serious cases, there might be brain damage or even something that has caused amnesia at some time in the past.

Pitted Nails
Skin diseases such as alopecia, dermatitis and psoriasis cause this formation. If the nail has just one or two deep purple pits, this can mean the person has recently had a shock to the system.

Beau Lines or 'Sea Waves'
Beau lines are like ridges or waves on the nail and they tell of a recent nail injury, a health condition or that the person has suffered a shock. On one hand, this can signify a serious condition such as a heart attack, malnutrition or trauma. They can also be left after a serious bout of influenza, an injury as a result of an accident, a slipped disc or other spinal problems, in fact anything else that is memorable. It could be a

relationship break-up, losing a job, a financial collapse or a very stressful time in general.

Lateral Wave Lines

If these lateral dents and ridges are stacked up, we know the owner has been in a state of repeated shock or trauma and could be very fragile. When found on the thumb of females, in multiple ridges, there could be hormonal or menstrual problems present. Another theory is there could be an imbalance with heart rhythms.

Central Ridges

When you see this formation on the nails, you will know the person will have been through a very bad time, as it represents repeated traumas and sometime a huge shock to the system. Arterial disease could also be present, or there could have been severe malnutrition or vitamin deficiency.

Fir-Tree Nails

Sometimes a raised ridge ends in an effect that slightly raises part of the nail end from the bed. The effect looks like a fir-tree at the end of the nail. This is a classic indication of heart trouble, often on the hands of an older person.

Mee Lines

White lines running horizontally across the nail are usually a clear sign of a recent trauma.

Nail Separation

When the nail starts to separate from the nail bed, it can denote anaemia or thyroid problems, or a fungal disease. This can sometimes arise after a bad reaction to drugs. Nail damage caused by false nails can also look similar, so it is best to ask the client about this first.

Terry's Nails

Named after Dr. Richard Terry, who completed a study of this condition in the 1950s, Terry's nails show the tips of the nails to be opaque with a darker band on the upper part of the nail. This can indicate heart failure, diabetes, liver disease and malnutrition and kidney problems.

Yellow Nails
This condition will be easy to spot, because of the colour. The person might be suffering with diabetes, jaundice, nerve injury or bronchitis. One or two discoloured nails might be the result of smoking, most likely the Jupiter and Saturn fingernails.

Brown Lined Nails
This can be quite a serious condition, but do check the person has not had a blow to the nail. If a brown or bluish line is seen running down the nail, this can indicate breast cancer, Addison's disease, melanoma or trauma.

Ridged Nails
Vertical ridges on the nails are usually harmless, and often nothing more than old age creeping up on the client. Sometime the nail can split, so a good nail restoring cream should be recommended. There could be a need to increase foods such as brown rice, sunflower seeds or sweet potatoes. Perhaps a small iron deficiency might be present, and often the owner will suffer from rheumatism or arthritis. These are all situations that arise from getting older and poor nutrition.

One Ridge Standing Out
Sometimes the nails as a whole aren't ridged, but there could be a couple of ridges that stand out on one or two nails. This suggests some kind of trauma to a bone or a muscle, cartilage, ligaments and tendons surrounding it. The actual finger will often point to the area in question. For instance, a problem with the neck or spine will show up on the thumb and/or Jupiter finger. Shoulders, hips, pelvis and central and lower spine will show up on the Saturn finger. Arms and legs will show up on the Apollo fingernail, and then ankles, wrists, hands and feet on the Mercury finger.

Black Spots
Black spots or small black smudgings on the nails can indicate impurities in the blood or a fungal infection.

Brittle Nails
Sometimes the nails will split and break before they are fully grown. It's a good idea to advise the person to wear rubber gloves when doing domestic chores or when handling bleach. If the nails are very pale, the

person could be anaemic. As mentioned before, brittle nails can also be caused by the subject's finances being out of control.

Reddish/Brown Spots
When a person has browny, reddish pits or marks on the nail, this is an indication of a folic acid deficiency or a lack of vitamin C.

Thin Black Lines
This can be quite a serious condition and it's one that's not often seen, but when present, it may indicate heart disease.

White Spots
White flecks or spots on the nails are a very common sight and they're usually harmless, often caused by blows that damage the nail to create this formation. In traditional palmistry, this can also indicate a shortage of calcium and zinc in the diet, but nowadays there is controversy about this theory. Sasha says this tends to be a common sight at the end of winter, so it seems to be partly caused by spending a lot of time indoors.

Arched White Line
Curved white lines can signify metal poisoning, e.g. lead.

Soft Nails/ Thin Nails
Soft, thin nails can denote malnutrition, endocrine problems and chronic arthritis.

21: The Thumb – Venus on the Hand

The thumb has about the same importance on the hand as the nose on your face. The thumb represents love, logic, and willpower.

» Love is represented by the base of the thumb, which becomes the Mount of Venus.
» Logic is represented by the lower phalange of the thumb.
» Willpower is represented by the top phalange, namely, the nail portion of the thumb.

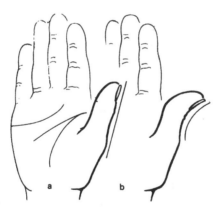

Stiff-Jointed Thumbs (a)

Owners of a stiff-jointed thumb will be less flexible and more rigid in their beliefs and they will take a lot of persuasion when asked to try something new. These people are less extravagant than those who have the supple-jointed thumb. The nearer the thumb clings to the side of the hand, especially if it cramps the palm, the more these subjects are inclined to seek financial security.

Those who are a little careful with money have thumbs that sit more closely and higher up on the hand. These types will also find it hard to move on from tradition, i.e. religious or political beliefs. They are also private individuals.

Supple or Flexible Thumb (b)
This represents a nature that is pliable and adaptable to others. Such subjects are broad-minded and often unconventional. The supple-jointed thumb also denotes generosity of mind, both in thought and money, and indicates a forgiving nature. These people are more extravagant than those who have the straight, firm-jointed thumb (a). Supple thumbed owners are impulsive and make instant decisions, often to be regretted later. They are fun, chatty and like "will-of the wisps," so you're never bored in their company.

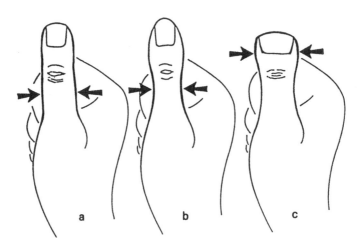

Straight Thumb (a)
What you see is what you get. They are kind hearted and hate to foist things upon others, so they don't make good sales people. They need plenty of peace and quiet to re-charge their batteries, and sometimes prefer to work solo to get out of the rat race. As they are self-contained, they won't mind being alone for days on end, as they love space to think, dream and be independent.

The Waisted Thumb (b)

To a great extent, these individuals rely on their instincts. Often they will do things on the spur of the moment, hoping that fate will give them a helping hand.

The Clubbed Thumb (the Murderer's Thumb) (c)

Through the centuries of palmistry, the clubbed thumb has been controversial. It is also called the elementary thumb. My long-dead grandmother would say that some of the thumbs she had seen looked as though they had been hit with a ten-pound lump hammer. If the rest of the fingers were markedly different, this formation would look out of place on the hand. These people seem to be somewhat resentful, possibly with good reason.

Flat Flexible Thumb

These types are often highly strung and will live on their nerves. Their constitutions are often delicate and they suffer from small and annoying health problems. Having a nervous disposition can hold them back from their true potential, so they will often be late starters.

Stiff Flat Thumb

These individuals are Victorian in outlook and a law unto themselves. They are hard workers, but they need to make an effort to take others into consideration.

Actor's Thumb

These thumbs are flexible and will turn back quite a long way. They are a common feature on the hands of actors and people who have to learn lines or presentation techniques. They can be seen on sales people and lecturers. Sometimes, these types can be rather full of themselves.

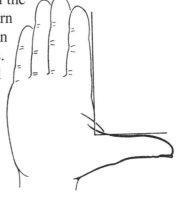

The Angles of the Thumb

When looking at a person's hand it is wise to take stock of the way it opens; therefore, the space between the Jupiter finger and the thumb is of great importance.

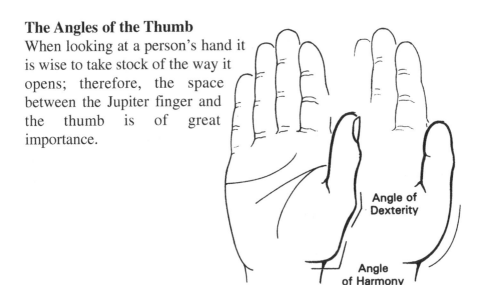

Angle of Dexterity

Angle of Harmony

When thumbs sit high on the palm, are placed close to the Jupiter finger, and are rigid, these types will have tunnel vision and unbending opinions. They can often be a law unto themselves.

22: The Phalanges

Every one of us has phalanges on our fingers, and they can give us a great deal of insight into a person's character. All are unique, and usually three will be present on each finger. The bottom phalange is nearest to the palm and then comes the middle one, with the top one being the phalange that bears the fingertips.

» The Top Phalange relates to mental abilities and the way we think about our lives.
» The Middle Phalange relates to practicality and the way we apply ourselves.
» The Bottom Phalange relates to basic needs, comfort and materialism.

Perfect Phalanges
These will be equal in length with no grilles, crosses or blemishes. The owners will be well balanced and successful in most walks of life. They will be hard working, kind and spiritual.

Thumb Phalanges
There are usually only two phalanges for the thumb. Sometimes there can be a third but this is not often seen. The top phalange of the thumb represents willpower, the second phalange concerns logic. A third phalange would indicate an unusual type of person.

Long Top Phalanges
Long top phalanges usually belong to the spiritual type of person, so philosophy, religion and metaphysical interests will be high on their agenda. They will be good as psychoanalyzing others, often scanning them with accuracy. On the down side, these people have to be careful not to become isolated or to withdraw into their own worlds, because

the gifts they have been given must be shared with others to help them to understand themselves more fully. They make excellent psychiatrists, clairvoyants, or reformers of society, so they can have a profound impact on those who come into their circle. Health wise, their nerves can sometime be a problem, and they must remember to eat properly!

Long Middle Phalanges
The owners of this type of phalange will be intellectual, witty and positive. They will often go into higher education as they get older, maybe taking a degree or going into teaching. The world is their oyster, as their heads rule their hearts. They are law abiding and responsible, and often take their attitude of responsibility into their place of work. The best professions for them could be medicine, science, business and law.

Long Bottom Phalanges
If all the bottom phalanges are longer than the other two, the owner's characteristics will be down to earth and he will deal with practical aspects of life very well, perhaps coming into the spiritual areas when he is older. His physical abilities will be strong, and hard work won't frighten him, as he will have plenty of energy for building, farming, gardening and semi-skilled employment. He prefers to follow than to lead and won't really enjoy being self-employed. If the palm is a fire palm, then self-employment is more likely. This person likes to be comfortable, both in the financial sense and in the sense of having a comfortable sofa and bed to relax into.

Short Top Phalanges
These people need to push themselves to study because learning and knowledge doesn't come easily to them. Even when reading a book, they will skim the pages or look into the back of the book for the ending. When doing a reading for this type, it is best to encourage them to take their time and be patient and then the small tasks will eventually become easier for them.

Short Middle Phalanges
When the middle phalanges are short there will be a need to stretch the mind to improve on practical skills. Often this type will go on to be quite creative, but will need to develop patience and perseverance.

They will want things done quickly, and they are inclined to be slapdash and untidy.

Short Bottom Phalanges
This type is inclined to be very materialistic and they can make money their god. If they are not wealthy, they must take care not to get into debt. They will love the latest fashion accessories and gadgets, and will like to keep up with the Jones's. The owners will need to bring action into their careers, as they can get stuck in a rut, staying in the same job for years.

Four Phalanges
This is an unusual thing to see, but when it does appear, it's most likely to be on the Mercury finger where it means that the person is good with figures, statistics and accountancy. This person could make a career in banking, or he may spend his working life dealing with contracts, legacies and mortgages. He could even spend some part of his life as an editor, designer, typesetter or formatter for publishing business. All this is really due to an aptitude for details and for reading meaning into statistics. He would make a good staff officer in the army where an understanding of logistics is the key to success. This person could become wealthy and then spend time or money helping charities. He is kind, courteous and fun loving.

Two Phalanges
Again this is a rare thing to see on anything other than the thumb. When it does appear, it's usually on the Mercury finger, but it could turn up on any finger. This subject has a good grasp of science, especially if the top phalange is the longer, and he may become quite famous whereby his pioneering skills could be a great help to science or medicine. If the lower phalange is the longer, the owner will have good commercial acumen. However, he will be very artistic and creative and he should be encouraged to use this more.

Fat or Thin Phalanges
Pleasantly plump top phalanges refer to a person who needs financial security and who likes to save money for a rainy day. He also craves secure relationships and will put a great deal of effort into marriage and family life. If all of the phalanges are plump, and especially if the fat is

hard-packed, the individual may be fond of food and drink, and he could have a lazy disposition.

Slim Phalanges
Slim phalanges belong on an active person who won't be easy going, as he has a nervous and restless disposition. Slim phalanges on the thumb represent a gentle soul who wants others to like him. He doesn't have much energy and he prefers not to do too much hard work.

The Jupiter Finger
This is probably the most important finger, as it relates to the person's ego, will and desire for success, along with leadership qualities and business or teaching ability. It has extremely strong connections to spirituality, and that is especially the case for the top (fingertip) phalange. I have gone into this finger in more detail than the others.

23: The Jupiter Finger

The Jupiter finger represents the person himself, his ego and the things he believes in, along with such things as leadership qualities and strength of character.

Jupiter Finger - Top Phalange

A vertical line

A vertical line here represents upstanding individuals who will always keep their word. If something needs doing, they will set about the task and achieve completion. They are always aware of their spiritual and psychic nature and try to live an honest life. As they are in the later stages of reincarnation, they influence and touch the hearts of those they meet.

A cross

In Vedic palmistry, there is a lot of superstition concerning a cross on the top phalange of Jupiter. Some say it is the mark of the devil, while others will say the owners will never achieve anything good in their lives and will subsequently ruin the lives of those around them. These individuals can lack vision and be young souls.

A star

A star with five points is a very good mark. It indicates the owners have a real mission in life and will help to improve the lives of others. These people become important and gain many spiritual rewards during their lifetimes. They have great wisdom and empathy with people, and a real understanding of the animal kingdom.

Two stars

One star is an uncommon formation but two stars are exceedingly rare. This mark belongs on the hands of those who are really old souls, who have great God-given wisdom. They can often be holy men, gurus and Mother Theresa types who will make a difference all over the world with their insight and knowledge.

A triangle
A triangle is an unusual mark and it should be perfectly formed so there is no mistake. This can be the sign of those that have been gifted with magic. High priestesses, mediums or theosophists might have this mark, as they are interested in all things pertaining to the spiritual or occult. They will live a good life and will certainly enlighten and inspire those they meet.

A square
The square represents protection from danger.

A circle
A circle is an uncommon mark that is a very good formation to have here. These folk will achieve tremendous things in their lives, and even when there is great struggle, they will succeed, because they have a deep belief in life and a strong faith in spiritual or religious matters.

An island
An island that is shaped like a crumpled leaf is not always a good sign. These individuals can get sidetracked in life. They won't think much about their spirituality and rarely achieve anything significant. Often they will take the easy path and hate to strive hard.

Dashes
Dashes on any of the top phalanges can represent fatigue for the individual. This is also a sign of stress at work or personal life. If the lines are red, we can assume their problems are recent. If the lines are faded, the events might have just passed.

A grille
A grille looks a little like a bit of woven cloth and is not a positive sign. The person may not have any faith or religion, and may lean too much on others.

Wavy lines
Wavy lines denote ambition. These people appear pleasant and they have many friends, but they may have a ruthless streak.

Dots
Dots or pitting on the tips of the fingers can indicate an underlying health problem, especially if there are dashes as well. The person's nerves could be bad and he could be suffering from acute fatigue. Sometimes you might advise the person to rest or have a good holiday to balance things out.

Jupiter Finger - Middle Phalange
A vertical line
This person will achieve much in life and will be well liked and respected. He has the interests of others at heart and he will make a good parent, partner or boss.

A horizontal line
This subject can change his mind at the drop of a hat.

A wavy line
A wavy line here represents ambition and a desire for recognition, along with a tendency to get others to do the work for the subject. He may have too many irons in the fire.

A cross
A cross can indicate potential success with writing or anything creative.

A star
A star is the mark of a saint or holy person who has wisdom and clarity of vision. Others seek him out to gain insight, even though the subject won't necessarily want to be in the public eye.

A square
A square foretells determination, strength and a driven nature. These types succeed in all they put their minds to. They make enemies but as this is a sign of protection, they will be saved from any real danger or from the envy of others.

A circle
A circle is the mark of success and a good and happy life. If these people are interested in art, their work could become well known.

A grille
These folk may have difficulty in keeping friends or relationships, and they may need help in becoming good parents.

Jupiter Finger - Bottom Phalange
A vertical Line
A vertical line here belongs on those who try hard to improve their personalities, and they don't allow their physical and worldly needs to control them. If there are multiple lines, they will make real headway and get to the top.

Wavy lines
This person tries hard to improve a difficult nature, but he never forgets a hurt.

Slanting lines
Slanting lines can indicate an inheritance and a wealthy lifestyle for the owner. This lucky person gets to enjoy the finest things and he may buy a holiday home abroad. He needs to watch his weight and his food intake as he can overdo things and damage his health.

A cross
A cross belongs on the hands of those who lack savoir-faire, and who can upset others by their lack of finesse.

A star
A star here is a sign of someone who may not always keep promises.

A square
I have seen this on younger folk who have had bad parents and no real guidance. They often have to bring themselves up or set their own standards.

A circle

A circle is one of the better marks to have on the bottom phalange and it denotes success.

A grille

A grille can show a fondness for drugs or drink.

24: The Saturn Finger

This finger relates to common sense, ambition, achievement, scientific ability, mathematical ability and success after a period of hard work. It seems to refer to putting down strong foundations in order to build something that will last. Thus marks here can denote struggles and hardship but also achievement as a result of keeping going.

Saturn Finger – Top Phalange

A vertical line
Sadness and melancholy, also possible self-absorption.

A cross
A lack of spirituality.

Wavy lines
Wavy lines indicate a lack of discipline and foresight.

A triangle
A triangle here brings success in love and career matters.

A star
Although these people may be in danger at times, they are protected, especially if there is a square around the star.

A circle
A circle is the best sign to have and represents a spiritual and mystical individual who will have great knowledge of things unseen. This is a very rare mark.

A square
A square is a sign of protection, so the individual usually lands on his feet.

A grille
A grille can mean disloyalty or of a period of unhappiness.

Saturn Finger - Middle Phalange
A vertical line
A strong clear vertical line is a good omen, representing great wisdom. This is a rare mark and I haven't come across it in my career.

A horizontal line
Horizontal lines laziness or temporary obstructions by others.

A cross
These are daring types who love to travel. Check the travel lines on the percussion side of the hand to see if there are any indications of troublesome journeys.

A star
In Vedic palmistry, a star is an unfortunate and rare mark, which can denote a serious accident, but it may be better not to tell the client this.

A square
A square on the middle phalange can be a warning to its owner to be careful and not take any chances, but while these folk are protected, it would be better for them not to tempt fate.

A circle
A circle is the sign of the psychic who could gain huge success and fame. In Vedic palmistry, this will be an old soul who has reincarnated to help others.

A triangle
A triangle is a rare mark and belongs on the hands of those who have a talent for psychic and magical matters. They love to study all things esoteric and will search deeply for the meanings of life, becoming visionaries and healers.

A grille
A grille indicates anxiety, so this person would benefit from meditation, hypnotherapy and counseling.

Saturn Finger - Bottom Phalange
A vertical line
A vertical line denotes courage and success in the law or the armed forces. A mass of vertical lines suggests careers that put the person in contact with the earth, such as horticulture, farming or mining. They are hard workers so they earn good money but they may be loners.

A slanting fork
Slanting forks depict characters that are hard to please, critical and fault finding. They can be lonely in old age.

A cross
On a woman's hand, a cross represents fertility problems, so you must also check the first Rascette of Venus to see if that is arched, because she might need fertility treatment.

Horizontal lines
Horizontal lines show those who are solitary and shy.

A grille
Grilles here belong on the hands of those with oodles of cash but they aren't generous with it.

A star
A star denotes a practical problem that is probably temporary.

A triangle
This denotes a love of learning and an aptitude for science.

A square
A square is a wonderful sign of protection against poverty.

A circle
A circle shows an ability to shine in the fields of research, science, and philosophy. These special people are leading lights and will help to pioneer new things.

25: The Apollo Finger

Apollo Finger - Top Phalange
A vertical line
Sadness.

Wavy lines
A lack of self-discipline and a disinclination to listen to others.

A cross
Luck with windfalls and inheritances.

A star
These folk learn the meaning of destiny and they have a cathartic impact upon others.

A triangle
These natives can charm the birds out of the trees.

A square
This person doesn't display good judgment when choosing his friends.

A circle
These people strive hard to improve themselves, and want to gather as much information as possible on subjects such as healing, clairvoyance and spiritual work. This is a sign of success and spiritual advancement.

A grille
The grille shows poor judgment.

Apollo Finger - Middle Phalange
A vertical line
A vertical line here is always nice to see, as the person will have a good heart and will be extremely kind.

Horizontal lines
A restless and rather shallow nature, they can't sit still or think deeply.

A thick slanting line
This can be an indicator of bad health to come. Check out other areas of the hand to confirm this. In ancient Vedic palmistry, this was considered to be a line of poison and treachery!

A cross
A cross here shows a daredevil nature and a fondness for challenging sports. They mix with like-minded friends and rarely settle to more serious pursuits.

A star
A temporary problem.

A square
These people shouldn't take chances.

A triangle
A triangle is a good sign, as these subjects are conscientious.

A circle
These individuals have a feel for future world events and they will be ahead of their time. Their predictions often come true.

A grille
A grille here can indicate ill luck, trials and tribulations. I often feel that these people are using their current incarnation to learn the lessons of three lives simultaneously.

Apollo Finger - Bottom Phalange
A vertical line
This denotes courage.

A slanting line
A slanting line is rare and can be seen on a military person's hand.

Multiple vertical lines
This person is tired or downhearted, but the situation is temporary.

Horizontal lines
These natives don't have a strong grip on reality.

A cross
A cross can signify a fertility problem. If on a man's hand, a low sperm count can be a possibility, or in modern-day palmistry, he might have undergone a vasectomy.

A star
A star doesn't augur well, and it can relate to violence in the home.

A triangle
A triangle represents clever types who have scientific brains but their friends can let them down.

A square
This person may feel that he is lacking something in his life at the time of the reading.

A circle
A circle suggests individuals who are working in research and scientific study. They have an air of authority and will gain great respect from others through their career.

A grille
These folk love money – maybe a little too much.

26: The Mercury Finger

Mercury Finger - Top Phalange

A vertical line
These owners will do well in most things in life; they have inventive minds and are they are often ahead of the game. These folk gain recognition and fame, and they may use their psychic abilities to enhance their lives.

Horizontal lines
Horizontal lines suggest the individual could be prone to jealousy or he may think a lot of himself.

A cross
A cross gives these types the gift of eloquence, and they can captivate an audience. They will be highly intuitive and able to see into the future.

A star
A star is a good sign, as the owners will have the gift for oration, teaching and lecturing.

A triangle
A triangle is a very special mark that indicates real psychic ability.

A square
This person will go into the deeper aspects of psychic work, and could become a medium or astrologer.

A circle
A circle is a positive sign for eloquence, popularity and success in media work.

A grille
This shows a deceptive natures and someone who may not keep promises.

Mercury Finger - Middle phalange
A vertical line
A vertical line reveals a talent for science, technology and research.

Horizontal lines
Horizontal lines denote a series of blockages. These folk have sharp minds and a talent for science but they may face delays in their careers or lives.

A cross
A cross on an in-bent Mercury finger can show criminal tendencies.

A star
A star belongs to a sharp operator.

A triangle
A triangle is a very special mark and the owners, after scientific work and exploration, will turn to the psychic and esoteric sciences later on in life and become quite psychic.

A square
A square warns of dishonesty, but the person can straighten himself out in time.

A circle
A circle denotes Honour for unusual and outstanding scientific work.

A grille
This person can blunder from one mistake to another.

A mass of vertical lines
A mass of vertical lines indicates hard work and overcoming difficulties in life. This also represents wisdom that comes with spiritual enlightenment.

Mercury Finger - Bottom Phalange
Vertical lines
This shows a struggle in life that may be a result of karma, but later life is better.

A mass of vertical lines
This person is temporarily short of money.

Horizontal lines
Horizontal lines represent temptations.

A cross
A cross shows the need for a good father figure or counselor.

A star
A star is rare for the bottom phalanges of Mercury, and I have only seen it once or twice in my career. The owners have the gift of eloquence and will captivate their audiences. They can be wonderful speakers and have creative natures, which will bring them blessings of success.

A triangle
A triangle is a good omen and the owners will have a lot of influence on others. They may become judges, barristers, or diplomats, because their negotiating abilities are exceptional.

A grille
Grilles suggest that the subject can be shady. He is a young soul.

A square
Secrecy.

A circle
An enterprising nature and a desire to help others.

27: Thumb Phalanges

A star
A star formation on the top phalange suggests a manipulative nature.

A cross
This person is easily led.

A triangle
A triangle is an exceptionally fortunate mark that represents academic types who shine in philosophy and scientific work.

A square
A square suggests stubbornness, but this also involves a logical, reasoning mind.

A circle
A circle denotes strong powers of concentration and someone who is logical about most matters. This brings great success.

A grille
Grilles are generally seen as obstacles.

Vertical lines
Vertical lines suggest people who can see both sides of the story and make good counselors.

Horizontal lines
This person needs to avoid being taken in by unscrupulous people.

Islands

Islands represent setbacks; the person ought to focus on his own needs and not allow others to walk all over him.

28: Palmar Loops

Palmar dermatoglyphics are much the same as fingerprints, in that they are formed when the person is still in the womb, and they don't change through life in the way that lines do.

However, they can break down into "string of pearls" formations if the person becomes ill, or if they become addicted to something.

Palmar Loops

Palmar loops can give us a fascinating glimpse into a person's character.

The Rajah Loop (see A)

This formation occurs between the Jupiter and Saturn finger and is quite rare. In Vedic palmistry, the person who is fortunate enough to have this is supposed to have a charmed life and is blessed with charisma, good looks, power and kudos. It can also mean high breeding with royal connections, or the person might have descended from important and powerful people. The person will have a regal look and good bearing, with fine taste in furnishings and food. When these people enter a room, there will be an air of importance about them and they will certainly have the "X factor".

I asked Sasha if she had any good stories about the rajah loop, as I had never seen one in my career, and what she told me was fascinating:

I was working at a large London festival of mind, body and spirit, where you do one reading after another fairly quickly. One day, two handsome, youngish men, both with the look of Seve Ballesteros about them, sat down together in front of me, although only one of them had booked a reading. They were so alike they were clearly brothers. My client thrust his hands out and after a quick look at the back of his hands and his fingernails, I turned his hand over and saw a rajah loop on each palm. Seeing one rajah loop is rare, but seeing two is almost unheard of. I glanced up and told my client he must have royal blood running in his veins. His eyebrows shot up and he said he and his brother were Dukes of Braganza, which meant they were members of the Portuguese royal family. I asked if I could see the other brother's hand and sure enough, he also carried a rajah loop on each hand.

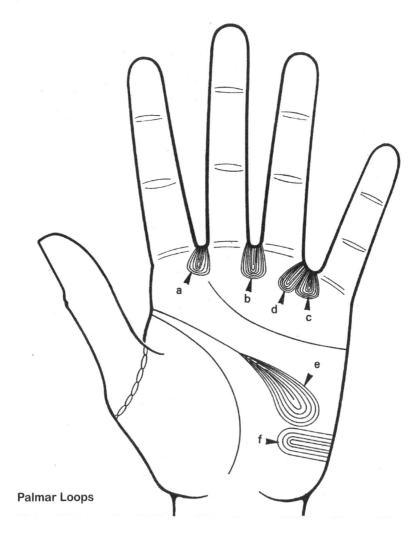

Palmar Loops

The Loop of Serious Intent (see B)
This is located between the Apollo and Saturn fingers. The owners will be studious, strong minded and reliable. They take life very seriously and try to make the best of themselves, especially in

education. There will be a quest for knowledge, and the more of it the better. My grandmother told me that this formation on the palm would rarely see its owner suffer with senile dementia, as their mind stays forever young and alert.

The Loop of Humour (see C)

This fits between the Mercury and Apollo fingers. These people are fun loving, mischievous and have a naughty sense of the ridiculous. They can cheer people up and bring a light-hearted atmosphere to any gathering. If the loop is high up on the hand, the owners will love animals and often subscribe to animal charities and events. If the loop has a central whorl, they are gifted in foreign languages and could find work as interpreters or even live abroad.

The Loop of Style or the Vanity Loop (see D)

This will be side by side with the Loop of Humour, between the Mercury and Apollo fingers. Although it has been known in the past as a sign of self-interest and vanity, modern day palmists tend to look on this as people with style who will like to look after themselves and who have a good eye for fashion, colour and interior design and decorating. Their creative streak is strong and they are inventive. On an artistic hand, the owner will probably have a career in fashion and design.

The Loop of Memory (see E)

This is found at the end of the headline and is usually very distinctive and quite large. The owner will have a memory like an elephant and will keep details from long ago stored in his head like a computer. If they are shown something just once, they will get the hang of it and never forget the procedure. They remember names and addresses of years gone by, and have the knack of clever and witty conversation. However, they can bear a grudge, as even negative thoughts will get stored away and never be forgotten.

The Loop of Imagination (see F)

This loop sits between the Luna Mount and the Mount of Mars, linking with psychic skills and imagination. These people will tend to rely on their own judgement, their motto being *Carpe diem...* seize the day!

They have an uncanny knack of reading your mind, and may have strong feelings of world events before they happen, especially if the loop has a whorl inside. Loops in the Luna area show a love of nature and outdoor pursuits like camping, canoeing, skiing and hiking.

29: The Rascettes

The rascettes are also known as *The Rascettes of Venus*, or the magic bracelets.

The Rascettes of Venus are found on the inside of the hand on the wrist, and they usually contain three lines (a). They can also be found arching upwards (b).

Each unbroken line is supposed to give its owner around thirty years of life. Sometimes a fourth line will be clearly visible, which foretells a very long life.

Arched Rascette
An arched rascette can sometimes be a sign of hard work and difficulties.

Triangular Rascette
A triangular rascette is not a good omen, as it can signify gynaecological problems for a female and possibly a hysterectomy at some time in the future or the past. If on a male hand, prostate trouble could be an issue. If the line is inflamed, the situation is current. If the triangle is smaller, then continence might be a problem.

Chained Rascette
A chained rascette is often the sign of ongoing family difficulties and health problems. The owner will tend to be tired and run down.

Fragmented Rascettes
Fragmented rascettes show a lack of foresight, ambition and a lack of organisational abilities. These types will leave things to the last minute.

Grilled Rascettes
Grilled rascettes are common on the hand, and can mean obstacles are in place. If twinned with an arched rascette, the diagnosis for female health might be complicated and deeper investigation may be needed. Scans or blood tests will be on the agenda.

» A cross in the rascette is usually an ill omen and can be a warning to watch for upsets and accidents. If on the non-dominant hand, this may have already happened. If the cross is surrounded by a square, the subject will be protected against disaster.

» Ascending lines between each of the rascettes are positive signs, because these people are doing well in their lives and making good progress.

» A square in the rascette area means the person has spiritual protection and real luck. They may live off the beaten track, or travel to unusual places, and they tend to live a charmed life.

» An eight-pointed star in the rascette is a very good omen, as it means the owner could see or experience something truly wonderful in their lives, often of a spiritual nature such as an angel, UFO, etc.

30: The Mouse

The Mouse is also known as the Vault.

The Mouse

Look at the back of the hand and close the thumb; you will see a pad of flesh on the hand next to the lower end of the thumb. In Vedic palmistry, this was studied closely to judge the vitality of the person. It can show the state of the person's lung functions and whether there are any respiratory problems.

Round Firm Mouse

Those with a round firm mouse have strong vitality and resistance to illness, with strong bones and muscles. They will be driven, boisterous, brave and full of optimism. They love to travel and get off the beaten track and may enjoy hunting, fishing and camping in remote places. They make good soldiers or athletic teachers. Nothing will faze them and they will enjoy life to the full. In matters of love, these types don't want a homebody, but a companion who is on the same level as them. Their libido will be high and sex will be very important. They will be too busy conquering the world to think much about their spiritual life.

Medium Mouse

Those who have a medium sized mouse are balanced individuals who will have a wide variety of interests. Their energy levels are normal, so they enjoy quiet and active times. They are good listeners and usually full of fun. As they get older, the owners will start to dwell on the bigger picture and will become seekers of knowledge. These subjects enjoy good health and usually have a long and happy life, providing they do things in moderation. In matters of the heart, communication will be very important to them. They are romantic and devoted, loving to be wined and dined, and will need a romantic partner to complete their lives.

Soft Mouse

People who have a soft or flaccid mouse tend to be weak-willed and easily led. Care must be taken with the lungs and they should never smoke cigarettes, as their legs and veins will pose a problem in later life, due to clogged arteries. As their lungs can be weak, they could suffer from such things as lung infections, bronchitis, emphysema and asthma. In romance, these individuals make many mistakes and often have failed relationships and marriages because they leap before they look, so they can end up confused and lonely in later life.

Flat Hard Mouse

Owners of a flat hard mouse have much to learn and, as the saying goes, they need to get out more! They have little physical energy and are likely to be untidy.

31: Mystic Markings

The hand holds many markings that contain secrets from ancient palmistry. To be fair, some are no more than superstitions handed down from the generations of gypsies, soothsayers and mystics, but many are uncannily accurate, as I have discovered in over thirty years as a working palmist.

Initials are often placed in the hands, and if an initial is on the non-dominant palm, then this is someone the subject already knows. However, when the initial is on the future palm, then this person has yet to come in to the client's life.

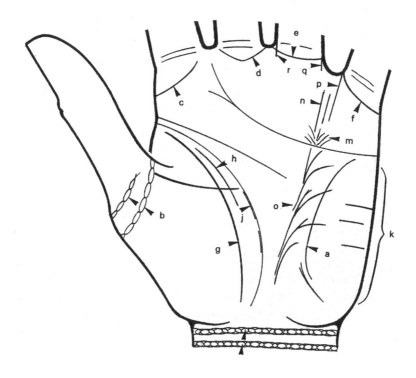

The Square
A square placed anywhere in the palm can be a mark of protection, especially if there is a cross within it. This can denote an accident that could have been worse than it was, or a time when the person's life was saved. The square can also represent talent for the owner, but they may lack courage to put their talents into action, so you might need to encourage them with this.

The Ring of Solomon (c)
The Ring of Solomon is found in a semi circle at the base of the Jupiter finger. It is rare, and considered to be very lucky. This formation tells us that the owner is psychic and will be gifted in all aspects of the occult and divination. Good luck and prosperity will bring happiness to the individual, who will always be in the right place at the right time.

The Ring of Saturn (d)
The Ring of Saturn sits just below the Saturn finger in a semi-circle. This is not a good thing to see, as it can portend difficulties for the owner. Common sense will not always be present and psychological problems could plague the person, hindering future judgement and possible future success.

The Ring of Apollo (e)
When this configuration is in place, it can indicate restricted areas of life associated with Apollo, which means the person is going through a time of deep unhappiness within the family and other personal relationships. With effort, they can change their lives and bring harmony.

The Ring of Mercury (f)
This can often be a sign that the subject will become a widow or widower. This line was present on Sasha's hand whilst she was living with her first husband; he then died of cancer. It faded after she married for a second time.

It is always worth bearing in mind that the lines on the hand can change and they can do so quite rapidly if the individual alters their way of going about things. Even unlucky marks, especially negative health lines, can miraculously disappear when the person turns over a new leaf or changes to a healthier and more active lifestyle.

Marks on the Hand

There are many marks that can appear independently on a palm or as part of a line. Each has a different meaning, and whilst it's impossible to remember them all, you can use this book to refer back to whenever you come across one of these. Here is a brief rundown of some of their meanings. Some of these marks stand alone on the hand, whilst others will be attached to a line on the hand.

Star

This can signify a recent shock or problem, especially if the star is reddish in colour. In Vedic palmistry, it can also be a sacred mark if found on certain areas of the hand. If, for instance, it is present in the quadrangle, the owner will be truly blessed.

Square

Means protection or restriction, depending upon the position of the square. For instance, a square on the heart line means the person's emotions or love life aren't flowing freely or happily. A square on a mount can represent protection from harm in whatever that mount represents.

Grille

A stand-alone mark that signifies severe trauma to some part of the body. For example, it will show up after an operation, but then fade away somewhat when the person recovers from the problem.

Pentagram

This is a rare sign of psychic or magical gifts. Often, the client can be a Wiccan witch if they have this mark.

Triangle or Half Diamond

When independent, this indicates talent, luck and inheritance. If the triangle is suspended under the head line however, it means the person has gone through, is going through, or will go through a feeling of imprisonment. This may be due to being stuck in an unpleasant job or a negative relationship. It can indicate an actual prison sentence.

Flag

A flag on the life line in Vedic palmistry can sometimes signify an inheritance. Where the flag is placed should give an indication of timing.

Cross
This is usually considered a negative sign in Vedic palmistry, such as accidents and misfortunes. In Western palmistry, if this is seen on the Luna or Neptune mount, protection can be given for sea travel and seasickness. On the Apollo mount, it can mean a windfall.

Cross in a Box
The cross represents a severe problem or danger, but the box shows the subject will be (or has been) protected from the worst effects. This configuration will often be present in life or death situations.

Circle
A circle is a rare sign and there can be some controversy with palmists. In Vedic palmistry it is a good omen, but in traditional palmistry, it means the opposite.

Chains and Islands
These always represent a string of bad luck, ill health and obstacles for the owner. Read the chapters on the lines to see what these mean in each case.

Slanting Line
Usually a slanting line crosses a major or a minor line. It can represent disruption in the individual's life, or it can denote a time when something breaks up completely. If the line is intermittent or dashed, the owner could be having start-stop scenarios.

Tassels
These can appear at the ends of the lines and show a weakening of that part of the person's body and vitality, sometimes due to illness or old age. For instance, a tassel on the head line can denote dementia, or if it is seen at the end of the life line, the person could have physical difficulties in later life.

Fork
This represents a parting of the ways.

Multiple Lines
This formation dissipates the strength of the line, which then splits itself into small parts. It can actually be a good thing, such as when it appears

on the fate lines signifying self-employment. Because there are multiple lines, the owner could have many irons in the fire, but will have to soldier on alone. Eventually their hard work will pay off.

Uplifting Lines
Lines that rise up from the major lines denote an upswing in the individual's circumstances, so this is always a fortunate thing to see.

Down Slope Lines
Lines that droop down from some of the major lines can be a negative configuration for the owner's life.

Wavy Lines
Waves on the line, or wavy lines around it, denote some form of weakness. It might be due to bad health, insomnia, or aspects of the person's work that are causing problems at the time of the reading.

Warts, Moles, Marks and Scars
You won't see an abundance of moles on the palm side of the hands, but when you do, they represent blocks of some sort, stopping the owner's progress. If there is a mole on the Mount of Venus, the subject could be having relationship problems. Warts are more common, and they also denote restrictions. Look at where they are placed on the hand to find the answers. When moles, warts, and scars are seen on the back of the hand, it could be someone else who is holding the person back. If the scars are old, it could be a past life issue.

Red Patches
Redness on one finger or one particular area of the hand shows a temporary feeling of frustration due to the behaviour of others or life in general. Check the finger in question or the area of the hand to see what's going on. If there is a red patch on a woman's palm on the percussion side of the hand, there might be hormonal problems or she could be going through the change of life. If the Neptune mount is red, there could be urinary infections or menstruation upsets. Often when the problems have subsided, the colour will go back to normal.

32: Relationship Styles

The Faithful Partner

Those who have earthy hands with little or no spaces between the fingers usually take things very seriously and will stick to a partner for life. A constant hand will have broad nails and fingers that can be a little inflexible. Study the head line to make sure there are no erratic lines present. A clear head line indicates a focused type of individual. The heart line should slope gently, and it should be free of fissures or erratic marks. If the line is a healthy pink colour with no tassels, the subject will be forgiving and nurturing.

The Deceptive Partner

In my career as a palmist, I have discovered the birth signs that find it hardest to settle down can be Sagittarius and Aries. Usually, they will have a typical fire hand (short fingers and a longer palm) and the hand will be firm and slightly red. Often, the Plain of Mars will be under-developed and the concavity a little deep. Fire palms are passionate and they like variety, so they can become bored when in a steady relationship. They take longer to mature and find true love, so they break many hearts along the way. When the Mount of Venus is over-developed and has a red tinge, the libido will be very high. The heart line will be a deeper red and might have chains and scratchy marks over it. Look under the Mercury finger for the attachment lines to see how many conquests there are and if there are forked lines, a divorce might already have occurred. The Mercury finger could incline sharply towards the Apollo finger, indicating a deceptive nature.

The Unsure Partner

This type of palm can either be Air or Water, and the Piscean or Gemini signs fall into this category. They yearn for love and a stable relationship, but can make bad choices because their hearts rule their heads. The Mount of Venus will be quite rounded, but perhaps a little flaccid. The fingers are long and pointed, which represents their dreamy and unrealistic nature. They seek ideal love that can only be found in books, so their heart line can have breaks and fissures, while the Girdle of Venus will be fragmented. Many will end up having a number of lovers, not through promiscuity, but through failed relationships or a continued search for something worthwhile. These types usually go through one or two divorces, so study the relationship lines on the Mercury Mount. Also look at the head line, because it could be bitty and broken, showing that the subject moves around and sets up home with one partner after another.

The Bossy and Abusive Partner
These types usually belong to the Fire and Air hands, and I have seen the signs more than once on Water hands. The Jupiter finger could have extra length and be wider than the other fingers. If the Lower Mars Mount is over-developed, the subject may have the unpleasant trait of lashing out both verbally and physically. A clubbed thumb is not a good thing to see, as it represents a quick, violent temper and child-like tantrums and sulks. If the head line is strong, red and chained, the individuals may have a sadistic nature with a real need to control their partners, children, siblings and parents. Check the hand is right for the body and not too short for the height or the makeup of the individual. The Mount of Venus could look too pronounced and over red.

The Weird Partner
Some of the Water hands can fall into this category, as they have secretive personalities, while small hands that are a little fiery can also suggest a strange nature.

ATTACHMENT AND CHILD LINES
Lines called attachment lines concern love relationships, marriage-type partnerships, actual marriages and important love affairs. Hands can't show marriage certificates or divorce paperwork, but they do signify emotional attachments, hence the name "attachment lines".

So, if you want to see how many marriages or serious relationships a person has had, or will have, you need to look closely at the percussion side of the hand between the heart line and the Mercury finger. These lines may be easier to read if you bend the Mercury finger slightly forward and look at the lines that enter the hand from the percussion side, on the area between the finger and the heart line.

Attachment lines

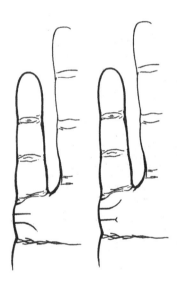

Widows and Widowers

One theory is that a line that loops down to touch the heart line can sometimes indicate widowhood. Other palmists say this drooping line has nothing to do with widowhood, as it merely shows the client is being "put upon" by his or her partner. Some say that the "widow line" runs upwards under the Mercury finger and "cups" the base of the finger. Attachment lines change direction fairly quickly, so if someone loses a partner who made them unhappy, and subsequently gets over the death easily and possibly moves on to another partner, the hand will change. The general feeling is that you should say very little on this subject, unless you know for certain that your client has already lost a partner through death or if the client already knows that their partner isn't likely to live much longer.

Difficulties in Relationships

A forked attachment line can indicate a split in the relationship, and possibly an actual divorce. If a line is faint and scratchy, the relationship will be undecided and difficult for the person. Sometimes you can see a small purple dot on a relationship line, and this does not auger well, as there might be violence or hardship within the union. An island on a relationship line can mean constant bickering between the couple, and they could part in time. The island can indicate another possibility, which is that the subject's partner is not in good health or is handicapped in some way.

Forks and islands

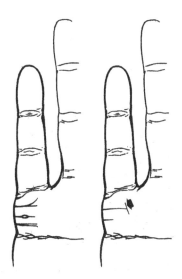

Multiple Lines

Sometimes when reading a hand you can see three lines: widowhood, divorce and relationship blips. The person might have gone through all three experiences, so it's a case of having the confidence to tactfully ask your client if this has happened to them.

Happy Marriages

When someone has been blessed with a loving marriage or relationship, there will be a straight, strong unbroken line. When a person is to be truly god blessed in marriage to a soul mate, there will be a straight line with another one tightly hugging it from below. In old-fashioned gypsy palmistry, this is called "spooning", and it's similar to the way that lovers cuddle into each other like teaspoons lying in a drawer. It is really rare to see this formation, and I have only witnessed it about five times in my working life as a palmist.

Child Lines
Child lines are found at the base of the Mercury mount and they run downwards, cutting through the attachment lines.

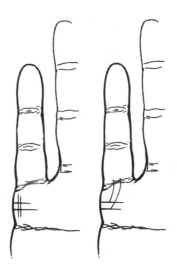

Traditionally, it is said that straight lines represent boys and slanting lines signify girls. I don't find this view completely accurate, and I can find myself being let down by the analysis. For instance, I have four straight lines, which would indicate sons, when in actual fact, I have just one child, a daughter. However, I once read for a very beautiful blond woman with the figure of a goddess. She had seven straight lines on her hand and my common sense told me not make a fool of myself by asking if she had seven sons! Later she revealed she had three sets of twin boys and had just had another baby boy. Even to my ears, it sounded too fantastic to be true, but it can happen!

Sasha says that multiple lines in this area can denote someone who loves children and looks after them for others, or someone who runs scout groups or teaches dance or sports to children. Another type that she has often come across is someone who has a deep affection for animals. I certainly love animals and have always kept pets, and there are many wild animals that come to my garden for love, attention and food.

Sickness on the Child Lines

If an island present on a children's line, the child could be prone to ill health. If there is a purple dot, it can be more sinister, as the child could be sexually abused or ill treated and bullied. One often wonders if the parent is responsible for this, or if someone else is perpetrating the deed without the parents' knowledge. It is a difficult situation to approach and in my reading, I would just hint that a child might need protecting and for the parent to be watchful of negative people around their children.

Miscarriages

These are generally found on the minor hand rather than the major one. One must be very careful when speaking to a woman about these matters. Sometimes a line will be faint and there could be a cross formation through the line, or the line may be fractured and bitty. When seen on the positive hand, it is best for you to keep that knowledge to yourself and not impart it to your client. You might make an incorrect analysis and frighten your client, or cause them unnecessary stress if they become pregnant in the future. Once again, the old saying comes to mind that, "when in doubt… say nowt!"

33: Spiritual and Psychic Palmistry

Many people love to hear about their psychic potential, and there are various indications of this in the hand. Information about this aspect of life has, in part, been handed down through my family, but also from esteemed palmists that I have met and from observing thousands of palms over the years.

Full Hand

When there are many lines in the palm, the person had a full life and he will experience difficult lessons, especially if the mounts of the hand are well formed. This brings wisdom, empathy, and great spiritual understanding. Their souls will be wise, and often they will help younger souls to reach a steadier pathway.

Widely Spaced Fingers
Individuals that have well spaced fingers have minds open to all things spiritual and esoteric.

Large Neptune Mount
The Neptune mount sits just above the wrists and if it is very round and plump the owner will be deep thinking and very tuned into the energies of the planet. I have often seen this formation on the hands of Wiccan witches and psychics. The animal kingdom will be important to them, and they love to be outside to soak up the vibration of their planet. They can sense impending disasters and predict where they will happen.

Large Luna Mount
Those whose fate lines start on Luna are guided by fate and they are keen to help others. Psychic palmists think these people are reincarnated for a special reason. On a scientific hand, these folks may invent something to help mankind. When seen on a medical hand, the owners will have been given pioneering skills to help dispel disease. A large Luna mount also represents psychic ability and a deep connection to moon magic.

The Phalanges
Vertical lines running up through the phalanges relate to subjects who work on improving their souls and their Karma. The ascending lines through the phalanges show that the owner has quite a hard life, but they gain much wisdom and knowledge from their experiences. They can uplift others and give hope to the desperate. If there is a strong medical striata on the Mount of Mercury, the owner will be interested in healing, crystals and the Bach Flower Remedies.

Sloping Head Line
When the headline slopes toward the percussion side of the palm, the owners will be spiritual. They seek knowledge through books, meditation and inward reflection. When the headline is too long or curved, these folk tend to have their heads in the air, seeking out gurus or other religious leaders to buoy up their faith. The ideas of others exert too much influence on them and they may slavishly follow others rather than working things out for themselves.

Dead straight head lines suggest individuals who aren't interested in religion or spirituality. They will concentrate more on science, business, money, travel, their appearance, their status, their homes, antiques, possessions or any number of other worldly matters.

Inner Life Line

Sometimes the hand will look as if it has an inner and outer life line. I have given the practical meaning to this earlier in the book, but I also believe the inner life line or "shadow line" on the perimeters of the Mount of Venus can tell us that the person has higher levels of protection. The subject could have a guardian angel or a spiritual guide. If the protection line starts from childhood, it can show the person's youth has been chequered and spiritual guardianship has been needed. If the line appears later down in the palm, the owner will have lived through some form of crisis or even a life and death situation, especially if there are grilles, gaps or crosses on the line.

Mercury Line, Health Line, Via Hepatica

There are several lines that can run up the hand towards the Mercury finger, and these can have a variety of names, depending upon the different styles of palmistry. These lines can indicate health problems in the hands of the subject, but just as often, they denote an interest in health and healing, either in the context of conventional medicine or the complementary variety. If you see this, also look for the Medical Striata. A curved line anywhere in this area suggests a psychic ability. People who have this line on the non-dominant hand will be born psychic, but they may not use their gift consciously. Those who have the line on the dominant hand will develop intuition at some point in their life, either deliberately or as a side effect of struggles during their lifetime. If there is a curved line somewhere in this area on both hands, the owners will make good use of their intuitive gifts.

The Mystic Cross

This should be placed in the middle of the Quadrangle, which is formed by the head line and the heart line, and the cross must be independent and not touching either of the lines. If you draw a line upwards from the centre of the cross, it should end between the Apollo and Saturn fingers. Sometimes the Mystic Cross will only be visible on one hand, but it really should be apparent in both hands. This mark sits in the middle of the Quadrangle and is very rare, as it might only be seen in one in four hundred hands. The owner would do well in tarot, palmistry or mediumistic work. This subject would be a very good judge of character.

This is the sign of the psychic or medium, and the owners will find it easy to link into the spirit world. Most of their lives will be closely linked to esoteric and holistic areas. If parents have a child with this fortunate sign, they should encourage the child to develop their skills at an early age. My own daughter, Leanna Greenaway, has this mark and has since gone on to write many books on different subjects linked to esoteric and Wiccan beliefs. From the age of three, she has been able to see angels, guides and pets that have passed away. Owners of the Mystic Cross may also have a strange electrical energy and their domestic appliances will break down quite frequently. Their auras are sensitive, so they get sudden electrical shocks from shopping trolleys or metal surfaces. Mystic Cross people can see the future in their dreams and they can see others' auras.

The Kundalini

Mystic cross owners often experience the Kundalini, and here is a short explanation.

The Kundalini is a Vedic concept. The idea is that our spiritual strength lies at the base of the spine. Vedic scholars depict this as a snake that they call "the sleeping serpent". The energy rises up the body and threads its way through the chakras until it exits the crown chakra (top of the head). The vibration from the body then connects with spiritual energy called Prana. The person experiences a crackling or electrical energy racing up through the spine. Once this is over, the Kundalini settles down and a feeling of well-being or healing ensues. In the modern world, we call this an MOT from the Angels.

34: Health and Hand Textures

Hand texture informs the palmist about the character and the current health of the client. I must stress that palmists should never try to be a doctor and diagnose anything, but it can be helpful to warn a client in a very tactful way about health matters and suggest a visit to their doctor.

Hold the person's hand, turn the palms upward and press the Mount of Venus and the other mounts on the hand with your forefinger. If these spring back quickly, this is a healthy hand.

Soft Hands

People with soft hands have a timid and quiet nature. They wish to please and have a gentle and forgiving soul. When reading for this type, it is wise to encourage them to have a little more backbone, because others can push them around.

Sick people and the elderly can have this type of skin texture. There could be a need to assess their diet, as there could be a vitamin deficiency present. We often see this condition with vegans and vegetarians. In younger women, this shows when they are overdoing the dieting.

Silky Hands

There will be a definite sheen to this hand, which will make it look as if the person has just rubbed in hand cream. Those with firm hands will be clever. They think with their heads rather than their hearts, and their intellect will carry them through life. These types are outstanding in their goals and achievements. If the hand is silky and soft, the owner might be prone to insomnia.

Wet Palms (Palmar Hydrosis)

This can be a tricky thing to identify, as the person might just be nervous at having their palm read.

Sweating palms often run in families. A more sinister side can suggest thyroid and febrile illnesses, and sometimes injuries and heart problems.

Pale Hands
This person will lack motivation, or they might be anaemic.

Red Hands
This suggests people with fiery natures, who are quick thinking and restless. The client may suffer from cirrhosis, or in some cases, from the results of heavy smoking.

Orange or Yellow Hands
I once saw this colour on the hands of a person who was a health freak and ate vast quantities of carrots! If the person isn't poisoning their system with carrots, yellow skin can indicate jaundice.

Grey-Blue Hands
This indicates circulatory and heart problems.

Red mottles on the Luna Mounts
This may indicate gynaecological problems, overactive thyroid and high blood pressure.

Blue-White Hands
This is linked with poor circulation and the person could feel more comfortable by living in a warmer climate. Sometimes there will be red or orange blotches present on the backs of the hand as well.

Pale Dry Hands
These people lack variety in their social life, or they may be dehydrated, or both.

Hard or "Wooden Hands"
Sometime people who work on the land will have this type of palm and they will be self-reliant and very tough. They will be critical of themselves and others, as they do not suffer fools gladly. If the person has a more sedentary job, their nature will be edgy and they can sometimes have a cruel streak. They can have bad nerves, be worriers, and usually suffer from rheumatic problems in later life.

Conclusion

In writing this book I wanted to record some of the interesting facts and phenomena that I have come across in my 30 years as a palmist. Some professional, traditional colleagues may find the subject matter runs against what they may have read elsewhere. All I can say is this book comes directly from my own experience of reading hands, and I hope you will find benefit and new knowledge from it.

Index

ZAMBEZI PUBLISHING LTD

We hope you have enjoyed reading this book. The Zambezi range of books includes titles by top level, internationally acknowledged authors on fresh, thought-provoking viewpoints in your favourite subjects. A common thread with all our books is the easy accessibility of content; we have no sleep-inducing tomes, just down-to-earth, easily digestible, credible books.

~~~~~

Please visit our website (www.zampub.com) to browse our full range of Lifestyle and Mind, Body & Spirit titles, and to discover what might spark your interest next...

~~~~~

Please note:-

Our books are available from good bookshops throughout the UK, but nowadays, no bookshop can hope to carry in stock more than a fraction of the books published each year (over 200,000 new titles were published in the UK last year!). However, most UK bookshops can order and supply our titles swiftly, in no more than a few days (within the UK).

You can also find all our books on amazon.co.uk, other UK internet bookshops, and many are also on amazon.com; sometimes under different titles and ISBNs. Look for the author's name.

Our website (www.zampub.com) also carries and sells our whole range, direct to you. If you prefer not to use the Internet for book purchases, you are welcome to contact us direct (our address is at the front of this book, and on our website) for pricing and payment methods.

You'll find more content at http://zampub.wordpress.com, and at our fiction / self-publishing site, Stellium Ltd, at www.stellium.co.uk and http://stellium.wordpress.com

Lightning Source UK Ltd.
Milton Keynes UK
UKOW06f2234130515

251491UK00001B/14/P

Keys *for*
ACCELERATED
CHANGE

Paulette Reed

Publishing House.
Published by XP Publishing
A department of Christian Services Association
P.O. Box 1017, Maricopa, Arizona 85139
www.XPpublishing.com

ISBN-13: 978-1-936101-66-5

Printed in Canada. For worldwide distribution.

ENDORSEMENT

My heart overflows with a good theme;
I address my verses to the King;
My tongue is the pen of a ready writer.

–Psalm 45:1–

DEDICATION

This book is dedicated to my
third born son

Ross Wyatt

who brings me tremendous love,

joy and laughter...

even when there's a hole in the bucket.

TABLE OF CONTENTS

INTRODUCTION

In times of transition, both within the church and the world, it is always good to have a solid rock to lean on – Jesus Christ. When everything around us seems to be swaying in the wind, when events in the world look as if they're getting darker, God is always firm and steadfast, a beautiful light. Even though God is *unchanging* and a firm foundation, He allows *constant change* in our lives. It is His desire that we grow in Christlikeness so we reflect His character in every aspect of who we are. One of the ways He forms Christ within us is through accelerated change.

We are living in times of accelerated change. Many jobs are changing, people are packing up and moving to different cities, trials and tests are coming at a much faster rate, and everything people have been comfortable with is shifting. If we're going to follow the cloud of God's glory, change is inevitable. Moving backward is impossible as we follow Him. Following God invites change, thus causing us to march forward to inherit the promises of God.

Our faith is often shaken to the core in times of transition. It's as if we're in a long, dark hallway – where our faith is being tried and tested. It is my desire to encourage you with the words committed to these pages to hold on and stand steadfast in the Lord. I want to place in your hands practical keys to help you get through the hallway of faith – to see your promises manifested on the other side. My intention in writing this book, as is my intention with all of my writing, is to encourage you in your walk with God. If you will just hold on through whatever test you're going through, I believe God is going to show up, deliver you, and bring you into everything He has promised you. Accelerated change brings accelerated fulfillment of promises. Believe Him for greater things and rest in His loving affection for you.

The reason we sense pressure in our lives, or feel as if we're being pushed through God's birth canal, is because it is His ultimate desire to form Christ in us. And one of the quickest ways to bring that inward transformation, that accelerated change, is through the trying of our faith. God is going to turn your tragedy into triumph and produce passion from the midst of your fiery trial. As you persevere, God's favor is about to shine on you, giving you victory and light where you have sat in bondage and deep darkness. God has created you with a unique destiny. His promises are being birthed in you, and through you, bringing you into the fulfillment of your God-given dreams as you grow in intimacy with Him and learn to wait for His perfect timing.

So I want to encourage you to stand the test of God's fire, knowing He is not changing and you will come out on the other side more purified and refined than you ever dreamed possible. May God bless you on your journey as you pursue His Presence, allowing Him to form Christ within you.

—Paulette Reed

1

THE AUTHOR OF CHANGE
NEVER CHANGES

Change Is Good

The church is in significant transition. The shifting can often feel like things are being shaken to the core. It can be both a happy yet scary time for many going through the process. It is as if people are being stretched like giant rubber bands on a slingshot, launched into new territories and realms with God. Change is difficult, but we must not fear the process.

The Divine Archer's aim is always perfect. He will not send you where He doesn't equip you. Sometimes tarnsition can be difficult; it's important to stay flexible and ready if the Lord brings in new wine, individually or corporately.

The river of God is continually moving. Not only is it always flowing, but it is also constantly generating new paths, being shaped and formed even as it continues to flow. In order for us to flow in the river of God, we must learn to flow with the rhythm of Heaven. If we stop changing and being transformed, we could stop growing in our Christian walk.

Think of how many times you've read the Word and remarked, "Wow, I've never seen that before!" It was revelation for now; it was a word for today. We must be very careful not to become locked into a belief system that never changes. God never changes (Malachi 3:6) and neither does His Word. But as Bill Johnson wrote in *Dreaming with God*, "The Scriptures are the basis for all 'hearing' from God. While God will not violate His Word, He often violates our understanding of His Word. Remember, God is bigger than His Book. The Bible does not contain God; it *reveals* Him." When we get locked into a specific belief system, revelation is no longer revelation and ceases to amaze us. You need to ask yourself if your capacity for the living Word is the same as it was ten years ago, or even two years ago, for that matter.

I often hear urgent prayer requests like, "God has asked me to do a specific thing, but I just don't know if I can fulfill that role." And I think to myself, "Nope, *you* can't fulfill that role. I can't, either. We are only dust, and to dust we shall return. But God can do it, for He can do anything!" This is because the same Spirit that raised Christ from the dead dwells within us, giving life to our mortal bodies through His Spirit (Romans 8:11).

It is exciting to watch people taking a leap of faith, stepping up to the plate, and eventually hitting a home-run for Jesus. Faith commands action! Change is good and must not be avoided.

Following God Requires Change

If we are to be followers of Christ, then change is inevitable. It is difficult, if not rebellious, to remain the same if we're truly walking with the Commander-in-Chief. Much like a soldier, with each battle won and feat accomplished, another star is placed on your shoulder. When you attain victory in a specific battle, you won't have to fight that same battle again. Change is bound to happen. Once you've conquered an enemy in a certain area of your life, it's then time to move on to the next battle that lies ahead.

We are constantly moving ahead as the army of God because we're advancing His Kingdom. As long as we keep marching, we are ever changing. Faith moves us ahead, step-by-step. And we will eventually walk into the Promised Land if we don't give up and lose heart. This doesn't mean there are no more battles to fight, only that we are reinforcing the victory already won by Christ. For why else are we here but to be "a good soldier of Christ Jesus" (2 Timothy 2:3)?

Jesus knew that following God requires change. In fact, one of the last commands of Jesus while on earth was to "Go..." (Matthew 28:19-20). This is why we often see an increase in the anointing as we go, moving with the cloud of God's Presence. The Lord promises that His grace will be sufficient and it will be there when we need it most, not a moment before or a moment too late. The river will part the second our big toe hits the water. How blessed we are to know that we can never travel beyond His care, "For the Lord your God is with you wherever you go" (Joshua 1:9).

Someone once said that faith is spelled r-i-s-k. Every time we step out, we are risking everything to follow God. We may not know exactly where we're going, or exactly where our pastor, leader, or church is headed.

But we do know Jesus, and He promises that knowing Him is enough. In John 14:5-7 we read:

> Thomas said to Him, "Lord, we do not know where You are going, how do we know the way?" Jesus said to him, "I am the way, and the truth, and the life; no one comes to the Father but through Me. If you had known Me, you would have known My Father also" (John 14:5-7).

Knowing Jesus is all we need in order to step out and follow His leading, because He is the way.

Abraham also stepped out in faith, risking everything, to follow God: "By faith Abraham, when he was called, obeyed by going out to a place which he was to receive for an inheritance; and he went out, not knowing where he was going" (Hebrews 11:8). He left everything that was comfortable because he trusted God, jeopardizing everything to obey Him.

Accelerated Change

Many in the body of Christ are experiencing accelerated change: a new job, a new location, a new ministry, and even a new perception of the church. The Lord wants to remind you that He is always with you; He will never leave you nor forsake you (Hebrews 13:5). Peeking out of that dark, protective cave seems a bit frightening at times. The brightness of the *Son* may cause you to squint after a long season of being hidden. Perhaps your wings feel a little weak as you emerge from the cocoon that enveloped you for so long. Remember, it's okay; you are not alone. The changeless Author is constantly bringing change into our lives.

David knew God's Presence according to Psalm 139. No matter how we feel or what we do, He is with us. Here's my paraphrase of Psalm 139:2-14:

> He knows when you sit and when you rise; He perceives your thoughts from afar. He discerns your going out and your lying down; He's familiar with all your ways. Before a word is on your tongue, He knows it completely.

> He hems you in – behind and before; He has laid His hand upon you. Such knowledge is too wonderful for you, too lofty for you to attain.

> Where can you go from His Spirit? Where can you flee from His Presence? If you go up to the Heavens, He is there; if you make your bed in the depths, He is there. If you rise on the wings

of the dawn, if you settle on the far side of the sea, even there His hand will guide you; His right hand will hold you fast.

If you say, "Surely the darkness will hide me and the light become night around me," even the darkness will not be dark to Him; the night will shine like the day, for darkness is as light to Him.

For He created your inmost being; He knit you together in your mother's womb. Praise Him because you are fearfully and wonderfully made; His works are wonderful; you know that full well.

The Lord knows there will be days when doubt will try to overcome your peace, but He will be right there, waiting to fill you with faith as you cry out to Him, "I do believe; help me overcome my unbelief!" (Mark 9:24 NIV). It is beneficial to experience change. Don't be afraid, because He is with you on the entire journey and through each step of the process.

Glory Doesn't Go Backward

It is exciting to know that change originates with the Creator of the universe. The Christian life is to be one of constant change: "But we all, with unveiled face, beholding as in a mirror the glory of the Lord, are being transformed into the same image from glory to glory, just as from the Lord, the Spirit" (2 Corinthians 3:18). We must keep on pressing forward as this process of transformation continues. Going backward is not an option. If we are not continually growing, we are dying. I love how a precious friend said it so powerfully, "We go from glory to glory; and glory doesn't go backward."

You may think you do not have the resources, time, money, abilities, or support to fulfill the huge God-breathed dream within you. It's okay, because Jesus said, "Blessed are the paupers in spirit" (Matthew 5:3 author's paraphrase). It is amazing to embrace the fact that in Heaven's economy, absolute futility is the bedrock of Kingdom authority. When we get beyond ourselves and realize we are nothing without Christ, it is a great place for Him to begin creating in us and through us. In the beginning God created when things were formless and empty (Genesis 1:1). And God continues to create today, longing to do so within you.

It's comforting to know in times of major transition that the Author of change never changes (Malachi 3:6). We must grow and continue to be changed into His image and likeness; yet, at the same time, He is changeless. "Jesus Christ is the same yesterday and today and forever" (Hebrews 13:8).

We cannot understand all of the change taking place in and around us. We don't lean on our own understanding but trust in the certainty of God, by faith. There are those who try to demand answers to questions that cannot be answered at this time. They want to be so sure and so well informed that they don't rely upon faith any longer. We need God's help, for without faith we cannot please the Father (Hebrews 11:6). When He returns, will He find faith on the earth? (Luke 18:8)

Fear of Uncertainty

We can never account for every single thing the Holy Spirit does. Jesus did so many things that even the whole world would not have room for the books if everything He did was written down (John 21:25). If we are one with Him, who is Truth, we shall not be deceived. May we never be like the Pharisees who suffered from excessive reasoning: "Some of them were looking for a reason to accuse Jesus, so they watched him closely" (Mark 3:2 NIV). Let us not forget that if wonders are explained, they cease to be wonders.

God knows fear will try to enter in as we risk everything to follow Him. That is why His love and the living Word cast out all fear. Elijah told the widow: "Fear not; go and do as thou hast said" (1 Kings 17:13 KJV). And God told Jacob: "I am God, the God of your father; do not be afraid to go" (Genesis 46:3). Fear of uncertainty must not stop us from Kingdom advancement.

Don't you think David's heart was racing with fear before he slew Goliath? I'm sure most of the Israelites felt fear in the face of the giant. Whether in the lion's den, the fiery furnace, or a season of tremendous change, most have experienced some fear when facing uncertainty. However, God provides the grace to manifest obedience in the face of fear. We are certain of Him, so we fulfill our assignment with courage.

Walking in Newness

For some of you, the Lord has already authored change but you're not walking in the newness of that change. In your mind you're still tied to the stake, going in circles around the same post. But you are free! It's time to soar. Jesus said of Himself, "If the Son makes you free, you will be free indeed" (John 8:36).

- You are free to say, "That's where I was five years ago, but the Master Teacher has shown me differently. It's time for a change."

- You are free to say, "I used to boast of poverty, but now I realize Christ came to give life abundantly."

- You are free to say, "I didn't realize worship and praise could be such an extravagant celebration at harvest time."

- You are free to say, "I don't understand all the supernatural ways of God, but I am a believer, not a doubter!"

- And you are free to say, "I don't agree with everything my brothers and sisters say or do, but I esteem them, honor them, and prefer them, obeying the second great commandment to love them as myself."

We are in a season of change. If we are not changing, we are sitting dormant, not fulfilling our God-given dreams and visions. God is the Author of change, though He never changes. He is the One who said: "For I, the Lord, do not change" (Malachi 3:6). If we want to remain in Him, we must learn to follow His river, constantly flowing and changing with it.

Let's pray:

Thank You for preparing the way for us as we prepare the way for You. It is exciting to know that a dream developed never leaves us where it found us. Thank You, Dream Giver, for changing us into what You want us to be – like Christ.

As we walk through the ever-changing kaleidoscope of life, may we stay focused on Your unchanging face. Change is difficult, but often the difficult thing is the right thing. Lord, You have promised, "He who tills his land will have plenty of bread" (Proverbs 12:11). Help us to believe Your dreams and give You our very best.

Every time we see the empty cross, may we remember that change is good. For You changed the cross from an instrument of death to a glorious symbol of life. Thank You for Your steadfastness during the changing of the guard. You are the Faithful One. Fill us with faith as we walk, not trusting our human sight. Truly, we love You, Precious Savior. Amen.

2

HE MAKES HIS SERVANTS
FLAMES OF FIRE

Instant Gratification

Our world insists on some things being accomplished quickly! The computer we purchased only a year ago needs more RAM and the microwave seems to take forever. And yes, we are living in an accelerated hour in the church, as well, where we will certainly witness many "suddenlies" of God.

One characteristic of the fire of God, however, defies our desire for instant gratification. Divine preparation always involves a time of waiting – not just waiting as if in a fast-food line, but really *waiting*. It may "appear" that some Christians are quickly catapulted into their destinies, but if you listen to their testimonies they, too, have been through the processes of the Lord.

There is a baptism for us to undergo, a season in the fire, before we're able to send the flame forth with relevance for the Kingdom of God. Jesus talked about this baptism in Luke 12:49-50: "I have come to cast fire upon the earth; and how I wish it were already kindled! But I have a baptism to undergo, and how distressed I am until it is accomplished!"

Preparation of the Lamp

It would do us well to ponder how God intends to send the fire around the world. As always, the Father loves to work through His precious daughters and sons, as we represent Jesus to the people. Abraham "carried the fire" when God told him to sacrifice his son (Genesis 22 NIV), implying that we are called to be torches who carry the fire of God's Presence. And just as John the Baptist was a "lamp that was burning and was shining" (John 5:35), we're also to be burning and shining lamps carrying God's glory and light throughout the earth.

In preparing for a sovereign move of God upon the earth, rest assured God will not hide your destiny *from* you. However, He may hide it *for* you. Solomon wrote, "It is the glory of God to conceal a matter, but the glory of kings is to search out a matter" (Proverbs 25:2). He will conceal your destiny until your response to preparation reveals that you are ready for manifestation. God may even ask us to lay our dream upon the altar for a season, as with Abraham and Isaac. He does this to see if we are serving the dream or the Dream Giver. But fear not, for He will return the dream unharmed once we pass the test of obedience.

It only makes sense that we are unable to carry the fire of God to the nations until we have first experienced the fiery furnace. We can impart nothing unless the Creator first deposits it within us. Consequently, the Father perfectly orchestrates our steps so we are blessed with our unique baptism of fire.

Baptism of Fire

What is the baptism Jesus says He must undergo before He brings fire upon the earth? I believe He is speaking of a baptism of agony, a baptism of the pain and anguish He was about to go through in Gethsemane.

For us, it speaks of a baptism of pain, anguish, and vicarious repentance.

Jesus said, "But I have a baptism to undergo, and how distressed I am until it is accomplished" (Luke 12:50). He was saying He was pent up, distressed, and not free to let the flame go forth until He endured this baptism. It wasn't quite yet time for Him to go through it, but He was distraught until the time came.

The baptism of fire is for everyone to go through. Jesus said, "For everyone will be salted with fire" (Mark 9:49). If a baptism of fire was necessary for Jesus, it will most certainly be necessary for all of His followers. The baptism of fire is difficult. However, we have not sweat drops of blood like our precious Savior did in the oil press, the Garden of Gethsemane. We must not despise the hour of testing in light of the love Jesus poured out on the cross.

Undergoing this baptism proclaims Jesus' and our willingness to drink the cup of bitterness, betrayal, and mental and spiritual suffering. This cup contains agony and loneliness. But He is assured His baptism of fire will not be in vain, and by implication assures us as well. Isaiah states, "After the suffering of his soul, he will see the light [of life] and be satisfied" (Isaiah 53:11

NIV). In other words, we can rest in the knowledge that this suffering will accomplish God's purposes within us. As you endure difficulties, challenges, or trials, you are to consider them purpose-driven fires suitable for the Master Craftsman. This is why James challenges us: "Consider it pure joy, my brothers, whenever you face trials of many kinds, because you know that the testing of your faith develops perseverance" (James 1:2-3 NIV).

Tested in the Fiery Furnace

Many Christians today are being tested, stretched, and tried. It's as if our God, whose eyes are like a blazing fire, is blowing His mighty wind from Heaven on His people. He's fanning smoldering wicks as He equips His servants to become flames of fire. We should not be surprised or amazed at this, for Paul writes that the believer's spiritual foundation will be tested by fire, revealing the endurance of their faith and love (1 Corinthians 3:13-15).

When we consider the fiery furnace, we immediately think of the story of Shadrach, Meshach, and Abednego, and how they trusted God to preserve them in the midst of their trial (Daniel 3:19-30).

The furnace of affliction and the process of refining are often compared to that of pottery being fired in a kiln. Genesis 11 speaks of bricks being baked in the building of the tower of Babel, and the brick kiln is also mentioned in Exodus 9:10 (AMP), Nahum 3:14 (NKJV), and 2 Samuel 12:31.

It's important to understand that the temperature of a kiln is always perfectly controlled. So it is with God's process of refining. He won't turn up the heat any higher than necessary in order to burn away impurities, thus producing transformation. Just as Shadrach, Meshach, and Abednego stood the test of fire because of the Spirit of the Lord being with them, so we are able to stand the tests of God's fire because He is with us, purifying us for our good and His glory.

Another noteworthy feature of a kiln is its insulation. Without proper insulation it is impossible to control the heat. The insulation is likened to being appropriately covered in the righteousness of God, cloaked in humility, and clothed in Christ Himself. It is when we are properly "insulated" that we can trust God in the fire, producing transformation, not cremation.

Don't run when entering a season of testing. Fleshly running can produce more oxygen, causing the flames to flare even hotter than what God ever intended. Allow only the breath of God do its work, letting Him control the heat. Stop, drop, and roll while asking Him, "What part of self needs to die in here?"

Tragedy into Triumph

Most of the impurities the fire burns away are obvious. For example, jealously, lust, pride, and greed cannot withstand the fire of God. Yet the Lord also uses what the opposition has thrown at us as fuel for the fire. God's strategy creates the opposite effect from what the enemy intended. Our Father is the champion of taking potential tragedy and transforming it into triumph! In doing so, we're able to stand and say, "To God be the glory!"

- As God longs to bring unity to His church – He may allow a season of the fiery pain of disunity.

- As God delights in igniting joy in the morning – He may allow sorrow for a night.

- As God wants to engender honor – He may allow a season of dishonor in the furnace.

31

- As God desires us to grow in grace – we may first experience a baptism of disfavor.

- As God longs to entrust us with Kingdom wealth according to His riches in glory – He may allow a season of walking through the fire of poverty.

- As God intends to exalt His servants – He may humble us in the flames of His furnace.

- As God begets us to be love – we may first experience the fiery darts of hatred.

It's important to remember that the enemy had Shadrach, Meshach, and Abednego bound when they were thrown into the furnace. However, it was in that very fire that Jesus set them free. Daniel writes that these three men, firmly tied, fell into the blazing furnace.

Then King Nebuchadnezzar leaped to his feet in amazement and asked his advisers, "Weren't there three men that we tied up and threw into the fire?" They replied, "Certainly, O king." He said, "Look! I see four men walking around in the fire, unbound and unharmed, and the fourth looks like a son of the gods." Nebuchadnezzar then approached the opening of the blazing furnace and shouted, "Shadrach, Meshach and

Abednego, servants of the Most High God, come out! Come here!"

> So Shadrach, Meshach and Abednego came out of the fire, and the satraps, prefects, governors and royal advisers crowded around them. They saw that the fire had not harmed their bodies, nor was a hair of their heads singed; their robes were not scorched, and there was no smell of fire on them.　　　—Daniel 3:26-27 (NIV)

Changed Through Trials

We don't just go from glory to glory, but we are changed from glory to glory. Second Corinthians 4:7 says, "But we have this treasure in earthen vessels, so that the surpassing greatness of the power will be of God and not from ourselves." When jars of clay go into the kiln, they are a brown, gooey consistency that doesn't have much strength or resistance. But after firing, a beautiful piece of pottery emerges, strong and translucent, aglow from the fire, crafted by the master potter's hands.

We need the refining fire if we are to become all God intends us to be. We need to see the church on fire, ignited for Christ Jesus. Since we know our God is a consuming fire, the Spirit of God lives and dwells in us, and we want to do only what we see the Father doing, should we not be a consuming fire also?

When we lay hands on someone and pray for them, they don't need to experience doctrine, they need to experience the fire and power of God! The world is waiting for a consuming fire to be manifest on the earth. It will be one that burns up all that is not of God: cancer cells, addictions, sicknesses, and diseases. That is a fire that will light up the world!

Fire Produces Passion

In addition to the purity created by the fire, the Holy Spirit also imparts a passion in the midst of the fire. This inner passion is for God's righteousness and for the advancement of His Kingdom.

Fire is an image used throughout the Bible to describe the inner nature of God's heart. I want to know the Father's heart and I want to have the Father's heart. Do you? To possess the Father's heart is to walk in the love of Jesus Christ and at the same time feel wrath against sin. If that involves a baptism of fire, then so be it!

Fire heals, cleanses, and purifies. The fire Jesus brings is holy and produces passion! It's in the fire that all of our false heroes and kings die, allowing us to see the Lord.

It is in the fire where the Son of God is manifested. We become more and more passionate for Him and His Kingdom because we realize we must cling to Him, walk with Him, and become one with Him, as exquisite crystal is fused in a kiln. It's all preparation for an eternal dwelling, recalled in Revelation 15:2: "And I saw something like a sea of glass mixed with fire, and those who had been victorious over the beast and his image and the number of his name, standing on the sea of glass, holding harps of God."

In the fire we truly realize that Jesus is all we will ever need. If you have been in the fire, are in the fire, or will be in the fire, be encouraged – you are not alone. The Savior of the world stands with you. The Rock of my salvation is in that fire with you. The Restorer, the King of Glory, the Son of God, the Word, the Rabbi, the True Light, my Shield, my High Tower, the Great Physician, the Ransom, the Peace Offering, the Ruler, the Refiner, and the Purifier is in there with you! "When you walk through the fire, you will not be scorched, nor will the flame burn you" (Isaiah 43:2).

Continue to be on guard, because "wet blankets" will attempt to drench the fire and extinguish the passion. Let me ask you this: What really happens when water is poured on the fire? I propose to you that in God's Kingdom it only fuels the fire! Elisha asked where the God of Elijah was (2 Kings 2:9-14). Let me tell you that He's in you. Don't let the enemy lie to you and use water to put out the fire of His Presence. Maintain your faith in the promises of God. Keep an attitude of gratitude, speaking truth so there is redemption. Use the water for fuel to fan the flames. And when the people see the fire, they'll say, "The Lord, He is God; the Lord, He is God" (1 Kings 18:39).

The Need for Perseverance

Once you've endured the fire and have received the passion, you must then persevere. You made it; you've come a long way. Jesus didn't quit at Gethsemane; He went all the way to crucifixion! Once you've endured the fiery furnace, you mustn't give up – you've come too far! You must set your heart like flint, ready to go all the way with God! It's in our own Gethsemane that we say, Father, "not my will, but thine, be done" (Luke 22:42 KJV).

We must allow the Lord to prepare us in the fire for the days ahead:

In the last days, God says, I will pour out my Spirit on all people. Your sons and daughters will prophesy, your young men will see visions, your old men will dream dreams. Even on my servants, both men and women, I will pour out my Spirit in those days, and they will prophesy. I will show wonders in the heavens above and signs on the earth below.   —Acts 2:17-19 (NIV)

May we allow the Lord to prepare us down here so we'll fit in up there when we meet our God, whose eyes are like flaming fire. Let Paul's words to Timothy be forever fixed in your mind and heart:

Fix this picture firmly in your mind: Jesus, descended from the line of David, raised from the dead. It's what you've heard from me all along. It's what I'm sitting in jail for right now – but God's Word isn't in jail! That's why I stick it out here – so that everyone God calls will get in on the salvation of Christ in all its glory. This is a sure thing:

If we die with him, we'll live with him;

If we stick it out with him, we'll rule with him;
If we turn our backs on him, he'll turn his back
on us;
If we give up on him, he does not give up – for
there's no way he can be false to himself.

—2 Timothy 2:8-13 (The Message)

Let's pray:

Lord, I know that You are good one hundred percent of the time. I know that You are kind and gracious. I thank You for the fiery furnace of affliction and trials You place me in. I know they are for my good and Your glory. I ask that You would help me to bear up under the afflictions and trials, continually being thankful and grateful to You for Your goodness in the midst of them.

I thank You that You turn all of our tragedy into triumph. I pray that Your refining fire would bring forth the gold from my life, that it would bring forth the purity and passion that You've deposited deep within.

God, remove everything from my life that isn't of You and produce a deep and lasting passion within my soul. Help me to love You with greater abandonment and a passion-filled fervor. Amen.

3

YOU SHALL BE

HIGHLY FAVORED

The Need for Favor and Grace

Throughout biblical history we see the need for favor and grace to be obtained from God. The Bible is full of people who found favor and grace with God. Here are a few examples: Noah found favor and grace in the eyes of the Lord (Genesis 6:1-8). Ruth found favor with Boaz, foreshadowing our relationship with Christ (Ruth 2:1-13). Israel will find grace with God (Jeremiah 31:1-14), while Stephen was a man full of God's grace and power, allowing him to do great wonders and miraculous signs among the people (Acts 6:8). Job prayed to God, found favor with Him, and then was eventually restored to his righteous state (Job 33:26). Finally, we see our tremendous need for God's favor and the declaration of its availability for us in Isaiah 61:1-2:

The Spirit of the Lord God is upon me,

Because the Lord has anointed me

To bring good news to the afflicted;

He has sent me to bind up the brokenhearted,

To proclaim liberty to captives

And freedom to prisoners;

To proclaim the favorable year of the Lord

And the day of vengeance of our God;

To comfort all who mourn.

As the world seems to be spinning out of control, we must remember certain things. The first is that oppression often increases before the long-awaited fulfillment of a promise. God is in control and has deliveries for us. He also has deliverers He places in our lives to assist us in praying for and spiritually birthing the dreams of God (Acts 7:17-18). It is also important to remember that we live by faith and not by sight (Hebrews 11:1), confident that God is determined to release favor to His church and secure us in the knowledge that the world will be blessed by it.

God's Spirit is upon us and He has anointed us to preach good tidings to the poor. He has sent us to heal the brokenhearted and proclaim liberty to the captives, to open the prison doors for those who are bound and to proclaim the favorable year of the Lord, all the while comforting those who mourn (Isaiah 61:1-2). The very mission of Jesus has become our mission. In the same way God sent Jesus, He now sends us: "Peace be with you; as the Father has sent Me, I also send you" (John 20:21).

The Favor of Mary

As we look at the favor Mary the mother of Jesus possessed, we see a shadow of how God wants to use our lives here on earth much like He used hers. It is incomprehensible to the finite mind that the Creator of the universe would humble Himself to become a helpless, totally dependent baby. We can see how our Heavenly Father wants us to be totally dependent upon Him in this great unfathomable act. We immediately take note of the fact that this baby could not have survived without being fed and nurtured by His mother and father. This too is indicative of how all children of God must be fed by their spiritual mothers and fathers.

It is as if there's an umbilical cord attaching Heaven and earth, with the Lord saying, "Feed my sheep" (John 21:17 NIV).

Being careful to keep the Holy Scripture sacred, we ask this question: Is it possible that some have been so careful to keep the Virgin Mary from becoming an icon that they have actually allowed the pendulum to swing too far in the other direction, missing what she was imparting to the church? After all, this woman of God carried in her womb the Rabbi, the Master Teacher, the Healer, the Miracle Worker, the Deliverer – the Messiah Himself. It was into Mary that God in human form was deposited with all of His glory and attributes. This was so that she may, in turn, pass that mantle down to all generations, to all who believe. Mary was truly favored by God.

Created to Deliver

While wrestling with the enemy once, I cried out to the Lord: "Lord, You are my Deliverer!" Immediately the voice of our Shepherd whispered to me, "And you are Mine." God has created His people to be deliverers. I'm not talking about deliverance in the sense of freedom from demons, though God has created us for that, too. I'm talking about delivery in the sense of having a baby and bringing forth long-awaited promises. God has created us to conceive, carry, and deliver on earth just as it is in Heaven. This deliverance takes place in the natural realm as well as the spiritual realm. I believe this is the year for heavenly favor; this is the year to see many dreams birthed!

As jars of clay, we're all carrying something within us. It could be burdens, sins, wounds, or other baggage. But the more the church becomes emptied of itself and its baggage, the more readily we can carry what God intended us to carry, the glory of God. Paul wrote that it was God "who has shone in our hearts to give the Light of the knowledge of the glory of God in the face of Christ." He then went on to point out that "we have this treasure in earthen vessels, so that the surpassing greatness of the power will be of God and not from ourselves" (2 Corinthians 4:6-7).

In His eyes we are virgins – pure and clothed in His righteousness. Consequently, He is hovering over us, looking for humble handmaidens and servants who are willing to carry the dreams of God from infancy to maturation, and who are also willing to carry the glory that will cover the earth.

Listen to Gabriel's proclamation to Mary as he is about to reveal that she is going to become pregnant with the Messiah:

Good morning!
You're beautiful with God's beauty,
Beautiful inside and out!
God be with you.

—Luke 1:28 (The Message)

The Scripture goes on to say that Mary was frightened at his coming, as some of you may be in regard to a call from God. This is particularly true if bondages have been placed on you because of gender, age, or even heritage. But Gabriel went on to say, "Mary, you have nothing to fear. God has a surprise for you: You will become pregnant and give birth to a son and call his name Jesus" (Luke 1:30-31 The Message). Fear was broken because God was about to show His favor to her and she was about to receive into her womb the very Promise of God.

We will only be raised into full stature as long as we are totally dependent upon the Father. He is the One who must do it, not us. In that place, we'll feed others even as Mary fed and nurtured Jesus. I believe the Lord wants to bring thousands out from their hiding places in the womb, out of prayer closets and into the light. It's time for spiritual babies to be conceived, for visions and dreams to be delivered.

This is a season when God's favor is going to come upon you in increasing measures. For those who believe and are prepared, continue to be humble and fear not, because God has a surprise for you. Do you believe God today? Do you believe He is able to do this? We must believe! Why would He plant seeds of His Spirit into an unreceptive womb?

Waiting in Transition

Waiting is tremendously difficult when we're expecting. It seemed exciting when the messenger came and said, "You will become pregnant and give birth!" Perhaps years ago, even as a child, God sent a messenger into your life - someone who planted a tiny seed, acknowledging your gifts or the call of God on your life. Incubating that life became increasingly difficult after the messenger left - when ridicule set in, when you felt alone, and when others didn't believe that the Holy One hovered over you.

45

Transition causes you to feel uncomfortable, restless, and off balance. Oftentimes you feel as if you're waking in the night, praying, pacing the floor, all the while waiting and waiting and waiting. We were okay with those inconveniences as long as the delivery date seemed right on our schedule. But when it seems that we're long overdue, the wait becomes almost unbearable! It is in that waiting time where trust in God's perfect timing is the most relevant. He works out all the details in that hidden place. Only He knows if your "baby" is black or white, male or female, short or tall, big or small. He is the One who has formed your dream in the womb and called it by name.

It sometimes may seem that nothing good can come out of our Nazareth. But God is not looking at our past or even the place of conception. He isn't looking at our resources, our money, or our talents. He's looking for a Bethlehem – a holy place to deliver His will, a humble place to cover His dreams in swaddling clothes, laying them in a protective manger until they grow, eventually entering the temple on their own.

You can't give up during this season of your life! There's no changing your mind when you're in the delivery room. God knows it's difficult, even showing us through the words of Hezekiah: "This day is a day of distress, rebuke and rejection; for children have come to birth and there is no strength to deliver" (2 Kings 19:3).

We must continually remember that it is God's strength that will deliver our dreams for the neighborhoods and the nations. In fact, He renews our strength as we wait on Him (Isaiah 40:31). So the longer we wait, the stronger we become. Rest assured, He is sending us helpers and midwives. Jesus never leaves us to carry the load alone. For, consider this: Even Jesus had Simon to help carry the cross! (Mark 15:21)

Birthing Dreams

Even while Mary was pregnant with the Savior, she still went to help out Elizabeth in her pregnancy. Luke writes, "Mary stayed with [Elizabeth] for about three months" (Luke 1:56). The Lord will often send you to serve other peoples' miracles before He delivers your own. Just because this happens doesn't mean God has given up on you – He will come through just as He promised. All of His promises are yes and amen (2 Corinthians 1:20). God asks, "Shall I bring to the point of birth and not give delivery?" (Isaiah 66:7-9)

Even if it appears your dream has suffered a spontaneous abortion, remember that the devil is a liar. Even if your "baby" seems too small, don't despise the day of small beginnings – even God became a baby. We are in the season of the restoration of all things, and it will be restored in accordance with God's Word (Acts 3:21).

Continue to watch closely as we approach an unprecedented harvest of souls in the coming days. If we look carefully, we can see a cloud the size of a man's hand and can sense the coming rain (reign of God). Therein lies your hope, even if you've tried and failed before. Continue to go back again and again until you see the dream God placed within you begin to come forth. "Love never fails" and never gives up (1 Corinthians 13:8).

Freedom Produces Good News

The closer we get to God releasing the great harvest, the stronger and more powerful the manifest Spirit of the Lord becomes. And we know that where the Spirit of the Lord is, there is liberty (2 Corinthians 3:17). Liberty sets us free from tradition and prejudice; it sets us free to receive and become messengers of God! It sets us free to run from the well and share the Good News with every person we see. News isn't truly news if it isn't shared. Liberty sets us free to go quickly and tell the dis-

ciples that Jesus has risen from the dead! Liberty allows
the entire army of God to fulfill the Great Commission, as all authority in Heaven and on earth has been
given to us. We'll go, making disciples of all nations,
baptizing and teaching them to obey everything God
has commanded.

Mary exclaimed with excitement after hearing the
news Gabriel told her:

I'm bursting with God-news;

I'm dancing the song of my Savior God.

God took one good look at me, and look what
happened—

I'm the most fortunate woman on earth!

What God has done for me will never be
forgotten, the God whose very name is holy, set
apart from all others.

His mercy flows in wave after wave on those who
are in awe before him.

He bared his arm and showed his strength,
scattered the bluffing braggarts.

He knocked tyrants off their high horses, pulled
victims out of the mud.

The starving poor sat down to a banquet; the callous rich were left out in the cold.

He embraced his chosen child, Israel; he remembered and piled on the mercies, piled them high.

It's exactly what he promised, beginning with Abraham and right up to now.

—Luke 1:46-55 (The Message)

Expectation is the greenhouse for miracles. Are you expecting great things from God today? It is good to remember the blessing in Psalm 90:17:

Let the favor of the Lord our God be upon us;
And confirm for us the work of our hands;
Yes, confirm the work of our hands.

May it be unto you as He has declared!

Let's pray:

God, I pray that You would help me to recognize the dormant dreams within me; the dreams I've forgotten about. Awaken those dreams once again today and cause them to come forth. I pray that my forgotten baby will rise up again and I would suddenly become pregnant with Your Word and Your promises for me.

I ask that Your favor would come upon me today and increase in exponential ways. Let me grow in favor with You and with men. Just as You poured out favor on so many people in the Bible, just as they found favor in Your sight, I ask that I would find the same amount of favor with You. God, cause my dream to be delivered during this season just as I help others in their delivery process as well.

Let me glorify You on earth just as You are in Heaven. Amen.

4

Pressure: The Birth Canal for the Dreams of God

"For those who have believed, labored, and loved
in the midst of persecution like our Savior,
He is about to deliver – MULTIPLE BIRTHS."

Birth Pangs

Speaking of end-time signs and wonders, Jesus said,
"But all these things are merely the beginning of birth
pangs" (Matthew 24:8). There is a season for everything we experience in life. Sometimes we get so overwhelmed with life's circumstances that we're not able to
tell how well we're doing. I want to encourage you today
by letting you know you are doing well. Step back, take

a breath, and rest in what Jesus is doing in your life. Focus, and don't forget the years of coaching from the Master Teacher.

There is a season for every part of life. There is a season to push, then a season to rest. There is a season to press through and a season to relax in God's Presence. But remember this: you are an overcomer! You must only keep your eyes on the focal point of life – Jesus. He is the only way.

I cannot begin to count the number of Christians who have shared about the tremendous spiritual warfare they've been experiencing lately, and about the pressure and the intensity of their walk with Christ. I'm sure you can sense it in your own walk as well.

The processes of God often remind me of the pressure cooker my mother used in preparing or preserving food. Pressure-cooking is a method using a sealed vessel that does not permit air or liquids to escape below a preset pressure. The intensity and high temperature completes the task quickly and purifies the precious commodities. This process is extremely efficient, but also a bit dangerous. There is just one tiny hole on the lid of the cooker that releases enough steam to prevent an explosion.

In certain seasons it feels as though we're the precious ones in the cooker. I want to encourage you to hold on – you're nearly ready to serve!

Do Not Waver in the Battle

One absolute in learning to live under pressure while giving birth is that we can't change our minds in the middle of labor pangs. We can't waver in the midst of the battle. There are many times we'd like to, but the Holy Ghost has set us up and there's no turning back. We only have to remain firm in our convictions to our Master.

The process of pressure-cooking is likened to a woman in intense labor during childbirth. As the force of the contractions increase, she'd love to say, "Excuse me, doctor, I've changed my mind. I'd really like to quit now. Things have just gotten too intense for me. No one told me it would be this messy, difficult, and painful. Gotta run now!" But in reality we know we must press through. Nothing can be delivered without that final push.

Jesus reminded us that the spirit is willing but the flesh is weak (Matthew 26:41). This is why it is necessary to watch and pray. It is easy to become fatigued from the battle, often feeling the weight of the warfare. We feel like we'll die if we keep pushing, but the truth is that we'll die if we *don't* push. There is always labor before birth, pain before delivery. One secret of bringing forth life is to not focus on the labor itself, as we'll magnify the pain, but remain focused on being a co-laborer with Christ. What an honor! He gave us His life, and we give Him ours. I don't know about you, but my life is all I have to offer Jesus as a sacrifice of my eternal love. Everything else is temporal.

I've heard many believers say the pressure is becoming so great it's almost debilitating. But prior to birth a baby is silent and still for twenty-four hours. If you're feeling a bit paralyzed, perhaps it's almost time for delivery, even of multiple births for some. Go ahead, be still and know that He is God (Psalm 46:10). The Lord is preparing a place for you as you prepare a place for Him.

Resisting Pain Is Resisting Gain

As the body groans with the onset of birth pangs, it seems to reject all that previously was. Everything that felt comfortable, safe, and warm seems to be coming to an end. And rightly so. There is massive change all around. The inevitably of this brings tension and perhaps even suffering. In fact, the rejection may seem so great that it can be comparable to stage three of transitional labor in natural childbirth, causing extreme pressure and even nausea. In birthing, it's the rejection and pressure that actually pushes out new life as we labor in love.

It is tough – no one ever said it would be easy. It is as if life is trying to cling to life, when the Lord is saying, "Let go! Let God! I want to multiply you. I want to bear fruit in your life. Life must beget life. Don't cling to something that's not even yours." In hearing this, we are to remember that we're stewards of everything and owners of nothing.

The long, dark birth canal of God's purposes seems to never end and the resistance is great. The enemy mocks us, saying, "You can't get in here!" (2 Samuel 5:6). He is only trying to throw confusion into the camp and abort God-ordained assignments. However, it is important to remember that it's God who comforts the afflicted and afflicts the comfortable. He loves us too much to allow us to be complacent. He will not leave us where we are, as we are.

Surviving God's Birth Canal

Spiritual birthing involves squeezing through a small, narrow space in order to launch us into a larger, expanded place. As we're squeezed, pressured, and pushed through the birth canal, we must examine what comes into view. Is it love, peace, patience, kindness, goodness, faithfulness, gentleness, and self-control? Many times we say we have the fruit of the Spirit and when it's time we'll use it to reach the world. But how do we really know if fruit is ripe until it's squeezed and tested? One of the best ways to tell if fruit is ready to be eaten is by its feel.

If we can't survive in the birth canal of God, we'll never make it when we're thrust out into the world. Perhaps we must remain in the dark, staying in a pressurized conduit a bit longer as the Holy Spirit continues to shape us into Christlikeness. It's here we're transformed into instruments who carry the Lord's glory throughout the earth. As mentioned above, perhaps we must stay in the pressure-cooker until we're tenderized with the meekness of Jesus Christ.

The secret to survival during the pressure process is to trust the Almighty, staying in peace and love. Yes, even when you don't have a clue what's at the end of the tunnel, your Father does. It is not just what we say but what we do that reveals the character of Christ within us. What seems like rejection from the body is actually what the Father is using to deliver His creations. We naturally draw near to Him as we suffer birth pangs. It is in this intimacy that all fear is cast out: "There is no fear in love; but perfect love casts out fear, because fear involves punishment, and the one who fears is not perfected in love" (1 John 4:18).

I'm always disappointed when I hear of women swearing while in natural childbirth. I think to myself, "Wow, you need all the help you can get right now. Not a good time to curse God." I've read that birthing is actually the closest experience there is in life to dying. Everything in us is filled with intensity – fighting, laboring, and struggling to hold onto something that's become a part of us. All the while God is saying, "I am about to make all things new! Push! Push into the future."

Let's refuse to go from drama to drama and crisis to crisis. Rather, let's go from peace to peace and glory to glory, believing all things work together for the good of those who love Christ Jesus and are called according to His purpose (Romans 8:28).

Expecting the Harvest

It is good to reflect often on the seeds we've sown and the labor we've experienced in our past. How can we help but smile at the goodness of God when remembering all He has done for us? We've counted the cost, we've tilled the fields, and the Lord has made our dreams grow.

We've been as farmers preparing for the harvest. They begin with fertile seed, the Creator gives living water, and the "Son" brings forth the growth. I believe the church is entering a season of fertility, a season of harvest. Consequently, she groans with birth pangs. For those who have believed, labored, and loved in the midst of persecution like our Savior, He is about to deliver multiple births.

As we anticipate the future of a glorious church, it can be likened to natural childbirth, knowing that we will not remember the pain once we're overcome with unspeakable joy at the sight of our dreams. The Lord declares, "For behold, I create new heavens and a new earth; And the former things will not be remembered or come to mind" (Isaiah 65:17).

I enjoy the way God describes this process through Paul's writing:

That's why I don't think there's any comparison between the present hard times and the coming good times. The created world itself can hardly wait for what's coming next. Everything in creation is being more or less held back. God reins it in until both creation and all the creatures are ready and can be released at the same moment into the glorious times ahead. Meanwhile, the joyful anticipation deepens.

— Romans 8:18-21 (The Message)

It will all be worth it as we continue to press through and push to the end.

Groaning for Future Glory

The whole earth is groaning under the pain of its iniquity. The lawlessness, evil, and darkness seem overwhelming at times. I don't think we can even imagine what it takes to usher in the new Heavens and new earth. But that is why we co-labor with Christ – He knows what it takes. That's why the Spirit Himself intercedes for us and builds us up, even as we're asleep.

Very recently I had a dream where Jesus came to me and kept saying, "Faint not, I'm coming soon. Faint not, I'm coming soon!" Fear not, for Christ is not overwhelmed with the world's circumstances – He has overcome the world and is coming soon!

Can you feel the pressure all around you? How can man comprehend the weight of the glory of God in the womb of God? We cannot. We must simply believe, anticipate, and rejoice. Paul went on to write:

> Around us we observe a pregnant creation. The difficult times of pain throughout the world are simply birth pangs. But it's not only around us; it's within us. The Spirit of God is arousing us within. We're also feeling the birth pangs. These sterile and barren bodies of ours are yearning for full deliverance. That is why waiting does not diminish us, any more than waiting diminishes a pregnant mother. We are enlarged in the waiting. We, of course, don't see what is enlarging us. But the longer we wait, the larger we become, and the more joyful our expectancy.
>
> — Romans 8:22-25 (The Message)

I want to encourage you to keep laboring for the harvest. It will all be gloriously worth it! At the end of a dark tunnel is the light, a rainbow covenant of love. Isaiah reminds us:

Get out of bed, Jerusalem! Wake up. Put your face in the sunlight. God's bright glory has risen for you. The whole earth is wrapped in darkness, all people sunk in deep darkness, but God rises on you, His sunrise glory breaks over you. Nations will come to your light, kings to your sunburst brightness. Look up! Look around! Watch as they gather, watch as they approach you: Your sons coming from great distances, your daughters carried by their nannies. When you see them coming you'll smile – big smiles! Your heart will swell and, yes, burst! All those people returning by sea for the reunion, a rich harvest of exiles gathered in from the nations!

— Isaiah 60:1-3 (The Message)

Let's pray:

Dear Heavenly Father, what an honor to be used as Your deliverers. You are ours and we are Yours. May You strip us of anything that is not of Jesus as we squeeze down the birth canal to reach our destinies in Christ. Your entire church groans as we groan; all the while the whole earth is groaning, waiting for the revealing of the sons and daughters of God. May you uphold us with Your mighty right hand.

As we leave what's familiar and secure, entering into a place we've never been before, we trust You, our King. Help us to stay in peace and love while under pressure, and not be moved as You jettison us from darkness into light, to the glorious wonder of Your precious Name. Amen.

5

Keys to Unlocking Your Hallway of Faith

Does it ever seem like you're headed somewhere and should be elsewhere, all the while feeling as if you're going nowhere? Are you waiting for doors to open but can't find the keys to unlock them? I believe I have good news for you. You may be in the hallway of faith.

Stuck in the Hallway

I recently had a dream about being in a long, narrow hallway that was filled with hundreds of believers. When I asked Holy Spirit for the interpretation of the dream, I felt like these believers were stuck in the hallway. They had stopped going forward and were trying to turn back from where they came from. They had become stuck in the process. I believe the Lord is up to something in this hour. We must continue moving forward, as He is about to show us the way, the truth, and the light!

As I was walking down that hallway, I remember having a sense of perplexity. I looked backward and then forward – waiting and wondering. As I peered ahead far enough, I realized the dimly lit hallway became brighter further off in the distance.

The next thing I knew, an honorable, international church leader joined me in the hallway. The leader was silent as she took my hand and we walked on together. As we continued, I could suddenly see several doors and one of them was open.

Going through the open door, we entered an office that housed a beautiful, large couch covered in exquisite gold brocade fabric. Sitting next to it was a loveseat in the process of being reupholstered in the same exquisite fabric as the couch. However, the task was only half done. I felt an amazing sense of peace in this office, recognizing it as a resting and dwelling place for the glory of God.

Hallway Symbolism

There is some very powerful imagery contained in the dream. I believe the length of the hallway indicates the duration of a period of transition, much like many of us are in today. The dimness of the light speaks of the degree and nature of revelation we receive along the way. The width of the hallway gives insight on the space available for maneuvering as we walk. The hallway was quite narrow in this dream. In fact, I felt as if I almost had to turn sideways to squeeze through. Even though it was a tight fit, I knew it was extremely important to go through, rather than trying to escape it or find some other way to get to the end. The narrowness seemed uncomfortable due to my restricted movement, but it actually kept me from going to the left or the right, compelling continuous transition through the hallway.

Walking down the hallway indicated progress, or living in the Spirit. It also seemed to represent a trip or traveling. I believe it was referring to the Great Commission: "Go therefore and make disciples of all the nations, baptizing them in the name of the Father and the Son and the Holy Spirit, teaching them to observe all that I commanded you; and lo, I am with you always, even to the end of the age" (Matthew 28:19-20).

When the cherished church leader took my hand, it was a symbol of strength, power, action, and possession. Hands are also instruments of work, service, and spirituality. They indicate ministry activities that fulfill God's Word and His will. The open door indicated a transition, or an opportunity in the midst of transition. While the office we entered represented a position of trust, where agency and representative powers are granted for one's service to another, it also represented the five-fold ministry: apostle, prophet, evangelist, pastor, and teacher (Ephesians 4:11-13).

The gold color of the beautiful cloth on the furniture represented the riches of the glory of God. Gold also symbolizes an enduring capacity of believers as overcomers, and an unchanging holiness, wisdom, and righteousness. The brocade is a fabric woven with an elaborate design, especially one having a raised overall pattern. In dream interpretation, a couch indicates a safe, comfortable place to sit and rest. Sitting can represent rulership, position, concentration, and receiving. It is furthermore a place of authority, power, business contract or agreement, and the Kingship of the Lord.

Lastly, a loveseat is a wide chair capable of, if not necessarily designed for, accommodating only two people.

The Obscure Hallway

The Lord redefines and adjusts the rules necessary for us to be changed from one degree of glory to another in the hallways of life. While we're in the corridor, the Holy Spirit gives us time to focus and pray for accurate direction. We may feel bewildered because we've never been this way before. But it is truly marvelous that the King of Glory takes our hand and teaches us a new way – a way we have not been before.

The hallways of God are periods of transition. They are pathways where the Lord connects the places we've been with the places we're destined for. Although we're not to look back, we are to never forget what has taken place in our past. We're not to forget where we have come from and how much God has done for us. We are to remain grateful in the midst of every circumstance, knowing that if we suffer with Jesus we shall also be glorified with Him. The Lord wants to build a bridge between your past and your future, catapulting you into your destiny.

Kingdom Keys

I want to give you some keys to unlock those doors at the end of your Heavenly Father's hallway. These are doors only God can open and no man can shut (Revelation 3:8). Receiving the keys of the Kingdom is crucial as the church moves forward into new offices and assignments. Here are some keys to be grasped in the coming days:

- There is to be no murmuring in the hallway. If we do murmur, we may end up in the hallway for forty years just as the Israelites were in the wilderness forty years. We must learn to not murmur, being thankful for all God is doing in our lives.

- We must stand on the promises of God. We can't see well in a dimly lit hallway, but we live by faith and not by sight (2 Corinthians 5:7).

- We must stay focused on the King – when He gets our attention He can adjust our vision and illuminate our path (Proverbs 4:18).

- Even though the hallway is tight, don't stop moving. It is easy to want to sit down in the hallways of life, in the transition times. We must keep moving, even if we only find ourselves pacing back and forth in intercession. It is important that an inner rest, a peace that passes human understanding, always accompanies the movement (Philippians 4:7).

♦ The two things to do in the hallway are to eat and drink of the living Word of God. The Word of God must become our nourishment, our life, and our sustenance. We become people who live from the very words of Heaven. Jesus knew the power of God's Word as nourishment. He replied to the enemy while being tempted: "It is written, 'MAN SHALL NOT LIVE ON BREAD ALONE, BUT ON EVERY WORD THAT PROCEEDS OUT OF THE MOUTH OF GOD' " (Matthew 4:4).

♦ I would encourage you to continue to press forward! Look back only briefly and only when prompted by the Holy Spirit, as He uses past experiences as connections to your future. Let the Master Potter mold your trials into bridges so you can cross over them and come into wholeness, as they cause you to walk in ever increasing holiness.

- We have to learn to trust Jesus completely with every aspect of our lives – He works in us for His will and His good purposes (Philippians 2:13). Everything that He begins in our lives He will bring to completion.

- It is vital that we know how to be adaptable, allowing the restoration process to have its complete work within us. The Lord cannot put old fabric in new wineskins or it will tear (Matthew 9:16-17). He will perfect love in us until it is complete. He never does anything halfway.

- You must find your identity in Christ when it seems you're alone in the hallways of life. God explains all things to His disciples privately (Mark 4:34). Whenever you feel alone, you must remember that you're never alone; He has promised to always be with you, even in the absence of an awareness of His Presence.

- You have to listen for your Shepherd's strategy, not stepping out until you have direction from Him. When in doubt, don't move. It is only as you hear His voice that you step out. Stay where you are until that point, because He has not told you to leave.

- You must persistently watch for the doors God opens, not what man opens. Many open doors can be presented to us, but we must learn to discern which one is opened by Him and which one our fellow man opens up. We must always choose the doors He opens.

- Follow the King! When we feel a bit squeezed in narrow places, it often compels us to seek the Lord. He then takes us by the hand and fills us with hope, expectation, and revelation.

- Lastly, we must always remember to remain grateful in the midst of contrary circumstances. As the door opens, we go through it without fear, only unspeakable gratitude and joy.

Your Personal Hallway of Faith

You might ask yourself where you are along the hallway: Are you in the beginning, the middle, or at the end? Understanding where you are in the hallway helps tremendously. When a footman knows the distance of a race, he's prepared to pace himself and use the keys he's learned as needed. He keeps his eye on the prize, knowing that tenacity is increasing as he receives glimpses of a radiant rainbow of light at the end of the corridor. Paul emphasized this as well:

> Do you not know that those who run in a race all run, but only one receives the prize? Run in such a way that you may win. Everyone who competes in the games exercises self-control in all things. They then do it to receive a perishable wreath, but we an imperishable. Therefore I run in such a way, as not without aim; I box in such a way, as not beating the air; but I discipline my body and make it my slave, so that, after I have preached to others, I myself will not be disqualified.
>
> —1 Corinthians 9:24-27

Faith becomes our personal possession in the hallways of life. It is in that place where Jesus increases patience, perspective, and purpose. If your hallway seems dimly lit right now, know that light shines the brightest when it's the darkest. Continually remember that you need both dark and light in order for your shadow to be cast, much like Peter's (Acts 5:12-16).

There were many who were weary in the hallway because they were at the end of one section of their journey with Jesus. Hold on a bit longer! You're a champion of the Most High God! Let Isaiah 57:10 speak life and nourishment to you today: "You were tired out by the length of your road, yet you did not say, 'It is hopeless.' You found renewed strength, Therefore you did not faint."

Oh, rejoice today. Again I say rejoice! The King is coming to take you by the hand and you shall walk as He walked, in the light of His glory. Jesus is the door of life; He is the open door. He is taking you from transition to position – a position in apostolic Christianity. Be encouraged today in the hallways of life. God is with you and is bringing change, making you more like Him!

Let's pray:

Dear Jesus, I ask that You would help me to stay steady, knowing You're always by my side, even when I don't sense Your nearness. Help me to live by faith and not by sight. I pray that You would give me unwavering confidence in Your goodness to me, knowing that You're leading me every step of my way.

I pray that You would help me to possess the keys to the Kingdom. Help me to keep moving forward, keep pressing on, and allow me to find my identity in You while I'm in the hallway of life.

I pray that You would help me to discern between doors which one is opened by You and which one men opened. I want to please You and do Your will. God, I trust You today. I lean not on my own understanding, but lean completely on You for everything I need. I trust You and Your Word – let it be my nourishment today. I ask these things in Jesus' name. Amen.

6

HEAVENLY WHIRLWINDS
BRINGING NEW ASSIGNMENTS

"When assignments change and the breakthrough angels show up, there are whirlwinds awaiting us."

Soaring on the Winds of Change

During this hour of restoration and acceleration in the church of Jesus Christ, the Holy Spirit is propelling us to live "on earth as it is in heaven" (Matthew 6:10). As the Master Artist paints us into circumstantial corners, our trust and faith are being forced to expand along with our tent pegs. We are realizing more and more that God is in control - that means we are not.

Control is only an illusion that robs us of total reliance on the Holy Spirit. Any attempt to control will also inhibit us from the ability to freely love as Jesus did.

God's love is revealed most clearly in Jesus' death on the cross. Paul reflected on this:

> For while we were still helpless, at the right time Christ died for the ungodly. For one will hardly die for a righteous man; though perhaps for the good man someone would dare even to die. But God demonstrates His own love toward us, in that while we were yet sinners, Christ died for us. —Romans 5:6-8

As the divine exchange continues – Jesus' life for ours – until the day of completion, our love for Him will grow with each passing day. This love will consume all of our hearts, souls, and minds. It will also motivate us to serve Him each day with greater zeal.

As we yield and hang onto the mighty hand of God, He picks us up and twirls us like a spinning toy top. He lifts us just like Phillip, taking us where He will, when He will, in His will (Acts 8:39-40). He then sets our feet upon holy ground while saying to us, "Occupy."

When assignments change and the angels of break-through show up, there are whirlwinds awaiting us bringing the awaited transition. We must live as a wheel-within-a-wheel, soaring with each spiritual storm developed by the Creator, believing there are angelic hosts waiting to assist and protect us, for the purpose of advancing the Kingdom of God. Do not resist the wind for it insists upon change and many will become un-stuck by its forcefulness. No matter what circumstances you are in, the Lord wants to lift you up and take you out – change is coming.

Preparation for Sending

As God is raising people into new positions at an unprecedented rate, we continue the crucial preparation process. Many Christians are downscaling, buying smaller homes, determining to get out of debt, and making other wise decisions. They are preparing themselves for rapid discipleship deployment – not even thinking about taking an extra tunic. The Lord may choose to send us across the street or across the world. Perhaps the King of Glory will open the gates and translate us to another continent, or He may pour out heavenly revelation to be written down for the benefit of the church. Whatever the charge, we are to be ready. The more we let go, the more we lay hold of Him (Galatians 2:20). And when the Lord speaks we can immediately say, "Here am I. Send me!" (Isaiah 6:8)

It's important to consider that people receiving those godsends must be prepared as well. As He sends gifts to His body – prophets, administrators, apostles, ministers of helps, pastors, evangelists, and teachers – it is important that we learn how to provide for them. Paul made this point when the Corinthians were not wanting to support him and others when they were preaching the gospel there:

> I am not speaking these things according to human judgment, am I? Or does not the Law also say these things? For it is written in the Law of Moses, "YOU SHALL NOT MUZZLE THE OX WHILE HE IS THRESHING." God is not concerned about oxen, is He? Or is He speaking altogether for our sake? Yes, for our sake it was written, because the plowman ought to plow in hope, and the thresher to thresh in hope of sharing the crops. If we sowed spiritual things in you, is it too much if we reap material things from you? If others share the right over you, do we not more? Nevertheless,

we did not use this right, but we endure all things so that we will cause no hindrance to the gospel of Christ.   — 1 Corinthians 9:8-12

We have to be prepared to take care of those whom the Lord sends us, for we always reap what we sow. This is an undeniable Kingdom principle. We must always honor God's gifts to the body so the house is not left desolate.

Heavenly Whirlwinds

As we look at whirlwinds as a type and shadow, we note the "suddenly" and "separation" that often accompanies them. Even though we learn to expect them, we never know when they will really show up. "As [Elijah and Elisha] were walking along and talking together, suddenly a chariot of fire and horses of fire appeared and separated the two of them, and Elijah went up to heaven in a whirlwind" (2 Kings 2:11 NIV).

When we've been prepared and trained by the Sower, then He can "take us up" to learn of Heaven and plant us wherever He chooses. Heavenly whirlwinds may catch us up geographically, spiritually, or emotionally; but no matter how they catch us up, God will do a work in us through them. The whirlwinds of God may seem uncomfortable at times, but we must learn to live in the eye of each Spirit-inspired storm. The Prince of Peace is the center of our being even when we seem swept away by life's circumstances.

God can use us more and more, being infused with His glory, if He can entrust us with each cyclone we encounter. The glory of God is contained in the wind, and He is the underlying, motivating force of life. He is always moving on our behalf, even when we may not realize it. He is continually going before us to divide the waters so we can cross over safely to the other side (2 Kings 2:14).

Whirlwinds are a vertical experience; they rise as incense, each one taking us closer to Heaven so we can flow with our supernatural Father. It's in the swirling where we are molded into Christlikeness, for God's way is in the whirlwind and the storm (Nahum 1:3).

Many of you may feel isolated and even forgotten at times. Does it seem as if none of your family or friends understand you, or even try to understand you? Don't lose heart! Though the ways of God seem mysterious and perplexing, they can be known with certainty. He is purposeful in all He does. He has not abandoned you nor left you behind. You are drenched in the anointing oil of His perfect plan and have been handpicked for

His special forces! God has tailored your current experience to evoke the sweet aroma of your worship. At the same time, He's training you to reign with Him.

Sometimes I hear people say, "Well, so-and-so is just too heavenly minded to be any earthly good." Personally, I've never met anyone like that. I have met many, however, who are too earthly minded to be any heavenly good. We are told to, "Set [our] mind on the things above, not on the things that are on earth" (Colossians 3:2). When we learn to please the Father and live on earth just as it is in Heaven, then His mighty power can and will be released.

Elijah pleased the Father with his life of faithfulness. It wasn't so much about his ascension as it was about his expectation for God to show up. He was intently watching for the whirlwinds of opportunity, not missing the opportunity to soar. Elijah didn't even have time to reason with his own intellect – he just believed and was consequently taken up, a type of promotion into God's Presence.

God is returning us to the basics of Christianity. We cry out, "Lord, teach us to pray!" He answers, "I did, a couple thousand years ago," referring to the prayer Jesus taught us to pray: for God's will to be done and His Kingdom to come on earth as it is in Heaven (Matthew 6:9-10). It is my desire to honor and cherish the Lord's Prayer – the perfect daily petition – as we decree its fulfillment. May we arise and shine because the light has come and arisen upon us (Isaiah 60:1).

Spiritual Eyes

When we learn to trust the storm winds of the Spirit of God, we also learn to trust our Heavenly Father to send help in the midst of them. It's when Elijah "was no more" that Elisha's dependence upon God greatly increased. He had to press on alone to see God's demonstration of power. Whether physical, moral, or mental, some may feel that separation is too difficult. But rejoice, for Jesus expounds all things to His disciples when He's alone with them (Mark 4:34). You may never grow more spiritually or emotionally than by transplantation and isolation. Pick up the mantle that fell to the ground in the glory wind and cross over the river!

Do you recall when Israel had been split into two different tribes, weakening her borders and clashing with her neighbors? It was then that Elisha, a prophet in his own right, was trapped and desperately needed God. It was at this time that he prayed for his servant's spiritual eyes to be opened to see the army of God which surrounded them. Elisha did not have time to debate doctrine or get caught in the daily routine of life. He needed the Helper! When Elisha's servant was afraid of the impending army, Elisha said to him, " 'Do not fear, for those who are with us are more than those who are with them.' Then Elisha prayed and said, 'O Lord, I pray, open his eyes that he may see.' And the Lord opened the servant's eyes and he saw; and behold, the mountain was full of horses and chariots of fire all around Elisha" (2 Kings 6:16-17).

I trust that our spiritual eyes will be opened, enabling us to see the hills full of horses and chariots of fire that are waiting and ready to protect us. In accordance with the Word of God, it appears there is an abundance of help available, for "the chariots of God are myriads, thousands upon thousands" (Psalm 68:17). We must know and believe the golden chariot is always with us and in us. It is in the holiest part of "the temple," and we always have access to it (1 Chronicles 28:18).

Let's pray:

Our Father in Heaven, "The sound of Your thunder was in the whirlwind; the lightnings lit up the world; the earth trembled and shook" (Psalm 77:18). Continue to show us

Your power, Father. We thank You for the whirlwinds that take us up to the heavenly realm with You, for they are full of Your glory. Let us have visitations like Elijah so we can live on earth as it is in Heaven. Even when Your fiery chariots separate us, we rejoice knowing they catch us up to You.

I pray that Your Kingdom would come, Your will be done. Please open our spiritual eyes that we might see far beyond what the five physical senses could ever perceive. We believe, Holy Father, that Your glory is in the whirlwinds. We believe that the hills are full of horses and chariots, protecting Your church as we march victoriously, occupying the land You've given us.

For Yours is the Kingdom and the power and the glory, both now and forever. Amen.

About the Author

Paulette Reed served for 20 years in church and social work before earning her degree in pastoral studies, psychology and evangelism in the late '90s. She served with the ministries of Francis Frangipane, Patricia King, and Joan Hunter, and now has her own ministry.

Paulette's writings have been published through *The Elijah List, Identity Network, XP Media* and *Joan Hunter Ministries*. Paulette was a co-author of *Extreme Degrees for Extreme Times* and has published her first book, *A Powerful Force*. Her website is www.propheticarrow.org.

Her heart's desire is to live a life of Christlikeness and to train, equip and mentor a life of faith toward our loving Heavenly Father. Her passion is to share the love of Christ, exhorting people to arise and shine! She is an accurate prophetess the Lord has raised up to bring hope and healing to the body of Christ, leading the lost to their First Love and the saved back to theirs.

Paulette highly cherishes her family and friends.

ALSO BY THE AUTHOR:

Advance into the full measure of the stature of Christ!
A Powerful Force is filled with prophetic insight, revelatory dreams, visions and divine encounters that describe the process of santification for all believers. Paulette has skillfully analyzed the ways of God as the "finisher of our faith." - Dr. Joan Hunter

---

Additional copies of Paulette Reed's books are available at: **propheticarrow.org**
and **XPmedia.com**

For bulk/wholesale prices for stores and ministries, you may also contact usaresource@xpmedia.com. In Canada: resource@xpmedia.com.

XPpublishing.com
A ministry of Christian Services Association